Your Guide to the
Revolution

Irish Mike

Order this book online at www.trafford.com
or email orders@trafford.com

Most Trafford titles are also available at major online book retailers.

Printed in the United States of America.

ISBN: 978-1-4120-5530-7 (sc)
ISBN: 978-1-4669-5848-7 (e)

Because of the dynamic nature of the Internet, any web addresses or links contained in
this book may have changed since publication and may no longer be valid. The views
expressed in this work are solely those of the author and do not necessarily reflect the
views of the publisher, and the publisher hereby disclaims any responsibility for them.

Any people depicted in stock imagery provided by Thinkstock are models,
and such images are being used for illustrative purposes only.
Certain stock imagery © Thinkstock.

Trafford rev. 04/30/2014

 www.trafford.com

North America & international
toll-free: 1 888 232 4444 (USA & Canada)
fax: 812 355 4082

If you are easily offended,

Fuck off.

BooK
1

Once again I cry for the world
In truth I cry for myself
In this I am the whole of the world
In this I am its death

What do you see when you look in the mirror.

Do you see evolution in action.

Or do you see a sheep in the herd.

Do you see a hero or a victim.

Do you see an Angel or a ghost.

Do you marvel at your reflection.

Do you turn yourself on.

Does the mirror ask you a question.

Can you strip away the layers of yourself.

Do you believe in magic.

Have you ever had an idea so radical and real you kept it to yourself.

Do you realise you are the only person who sees the world as you do.

Is there a song that makes you cry.

Are you as crazy as you really are or just as you'd like to be.

Self doubt comes from without not within.
Fear is an expression of memory.
Power is an expression of internal strength
but tears can be also.
Is your heart beating to the drum of the
world.
Do your eyes drift skyward.
What if today was the first time you saw
clouds.
What if today was the last day of your life.
What if everything you believe in turned
out to be wrong.
Nothing is ever lost only hidden.
Time is relative to how you spend it.
Does the existence of a concept mean it is
possible.
Would it feel the same if you were the
opposite sex.
Can you hear the voice in your mind.
Is it your friend.

Are you a teenager if so good on you why your energy that incredible creative driven rampage of desecration and destruction where everything is fucked the world as it is only deserves to be torn down thrashed and forgot about I agree do it the respect I have for that frame of mind you are forcing a change do not become complacent you make us ask what the fuck is wrong with the world.

If you're no longer a teenager don't worry and more importantly don't worry about them don't try to control them don't try to understand them just hold onto your ass and watch the future of humanity take shape hold onto your ass and hope you aren't crushed in its wake an unpopular opinion I would think but who gives a fuck opinions are only as popular as the people who hold them.

Energy yes the ripping kicking screaming howling raving half crazy rampaging never changing hair raising fire walking bungee jumping free falling cliff hanging always laughing and then just sleeping ball of energy that exists in you even now as we count off the days in decades the last unexplored place on the planet is the playground of your mind.

Wanna set fire to myself to you to the world seeing always feeling always healing always believing in the one truth that holds us together the truth of being alive despite all the odds not just alive but alive and fucking kickin bitchin our way through this amazing rat race we have created for ourselves and isn't it amazing to behold.

We are only beginning to achieve the things in life that our minds can conceive soon we will speak of global opinion in the way we now speak of local opinion if you are pessimistic about the future of this race I'd suggest a good fisting to clear your mind and where is your mind does thought really only exist in the brain as we are told today.

I disagree if your entire body experiences something your entire body remembers hark the dawning of a new age of enlightenment the old rules no longer apply the butchery and savagery of the last thousand years will soon fade in our memories we have taken war to its ultimate state now it's just boring the future is yours mine ours to take and remake as we actually want to.

No longer victims of circumstance we but bringers of hope and imagination to the next generation bring it on let new experience be our goal the establishment is beginning to crumble the ones who created the Hell that was the close of the 20th Century will all soon be dead and with them the stupidity of that era raise your glasses as you put them in the ground and drink to the future unfolding.

Freedom is the new religion healing is the future now seeing is as feeling now thinking is the planet now growing is the species now water is just flowing now trees just keep on growing now waves just keep on rolling now drums just keep on drumming now Earth just keeps on spinning now like the ones who're winning now 'cause they keep on living now at their best forever now so who are you pick a number antagonist protagonist anarchist optimist realist defeatist piss artist winner loser taker giver keeper thinker seer all of these and none staring at the future down the barrel of gun no not I said the man freedom fighter renegade writer seeing through the clouded layers to a place always brighter where a man can touch the stars leapfrog over galaxies whose beauty brings him to his knees.

On his knees begging let me please remain from now until the Sun no longer burns and the Earth no longer turns the truth of beauty stands alone where once we saw clouds and dust but now we see ourselves we must continue looking always for the one who brought the light before and whose heart beats evermore and on down through time and through your mind always there just ahead of where you are always saying come not far to the place you look behind the layers that are built to blind you to the miracle of humankind where to turn where to start to find the place within your heart where all is real and just itself not needing to twist and turn inside-out and upside-down to make sense of what you've found but only to look and feel the truth and beauty of the real.

Where magic grows just underneath the surface and beneath your feet waiting just out of reach for you to stretch out your hand and take your share of Neverland where you know you've been before if only you could find the door that leads you back to where and when it all began and will end in truth and beauty once again and so we stand and shout and scream we never see what's in between the oceans and the sky as all the questions burning why why is this why are we who brought us to this misery that we often call our lives but now and then we see a path we've walked before the world was old in a dreaming place we were not caring why just being there in the rocks and in the air there lives a strength beyond compare of which you are part though not aware.

And of this strength pure beauty holds one's heart entwined with strands of gold the memory of that when the world was young and imagining was all you done dreaming trips beyond the Sun through galaxies infinium whose beauty just makes tears run and knowing it goes on and on past thought of time or idiom intelligence out here is useless with far more stars than there could be numbers distance fiction in an instant you travel a ten light year long mission blink you're home a blue-green planet blink again you are a comet on a random trajectory to the far off corners of the most amazing galaxy that you've ever seen but only one of many and wherever you go you're always at the centre out here things are different out here nothing matters.

The ones who watch the ones who fail you've had your chance but not for real beneath the surface beauty lies in all men's hands and all men's eyes on every day with every Sun the Moon reflects the Earth as one with all its treasures shining there on men who could not even care but far prefer looking in fearing for his life of sin and asking why he feels this way ignore the glory of the day and sit instead in dark and shade and wonder why his self made cage fits so well and doesn't age as he still does with every day it's never too late to open your mind accept the mysteries that you find as part of you and what you are not just yourself but something more of that which lies behind the door and waits for you to just break through.

The shadows that we always use to hide us from the one who's true to himself and to you not caring if you win or lose only that you play the game true to yourself and your name and taking time to help another for every man could be your brother though you've never met on Earth before there is an ocean with no shore where Angels sail and laugh at when the Earth they knew was ruled by men all far too busy to even see the beauty and the mystery that lives in all of you and me and though I live with these men who don't care how and don't care when the show began and will end in truth and beauty once again guaranteed I won't wear blinkers as open minded as the children who know there is so much to learn with every step 'round every turn.

And so we wait and pass the day fearing of the kiss of clay when man returns to his mother and to the sky he once lived under becoming just a drop of rain the ocean then a cloud again down to where the Earth is warm or in the eye of a summer storm a leaf perhaps for just a day a rabbit or a bird of prey a planet with a thousand moons never tiring of the change from this to that through every place and every plane that could exist is there a place where one could say this is the end and turn away back to where from once you came but will never be the same because you've been beyond the Sun and seen the moons of Linium spin faster than your mind can run and was it real or just for fun who cares because the memory's there a mirror hanging in the air.

There is a certain state of grace we all possess and can't erase a memory of that time the world was young as was your mind staring through with heart laid bare by truth and beauty everywhere the world's alive but are you on your knees pull up a pew time to pray time to die no not me no not I Irish Mike is my name I'm here to win this stupid game while on my way break every rule you see I'm from a different school I won't be told what to do how to behave when to grow up do I care do I fuck join me in this worthy fight we will prevail 'cause we are right on the money place your bets take a stand for the future in your hand an end to war an end to famine an end to poverty no longer fantasy we have the means we have the knowledge join with me let's make it happen.

Clarity majesty energy longevity are yours if only
you could see the beauty and the mystery that is the
person that you are a blade of grass a tiny stone knows
everything that could be known but how you ask do you
know the truth of beauty stands alone in your eyes and
in your bones ask not why am I here just accept the fact
and open your ears to the beating heart of the world the
sound of rain as it falls your neighbours fucking behind
the walls the sound of cars as they rush past the wind as
it blows or blasts the birds as they come out to play in the
glory of the day not caring why the Sun came up just that
it did that was enough why is it that we live this way and
teach our kids to live the same the hollow shells we call
ourselves walking shadows of what we were when the
world was young we were pure.

Who cares for you and all your ills when everybody just
pops pills as if the saviour was contained within look to
yourself for a cure strength inside the heart that's pure
like gold it shines and in your mind is the key to that
fucking door that leads to wonder evermore run don't
walk it's all uphill but what to fuck you'll get there and
then you'll see the beauty and the mystery screaming
rocks and screaming trees screaming suns and galaxies
all part of you and part of me relax child your time will
come you'll feel the beauty of the Sun and falling softly to
your knees such beauty as the mystery allows itself to be
revealed to anyone who cares to know there is an ocean
with no shore I've seen it once or maybe more there's
healing in the waters there the mirror hanging in the air
will show the way if you dare.

And lift your head just slowly then the Sun reflects the
light within and burns away imagined sin so then stand
up greet the day the shadow quickly melts away the
morning sounds as they play your heart strings favourite
melody and do you think you're the only one who sees
the world and feels it's wrong how could this be what
have we done to live a life bereft of fun for pleasure is
all that matters deny yourself the mirror shatters a billion
fragments of life in tatters love this life for all it is walk tall
and never hang your head the world awaits the world
awaits in each of you there is a spark part of the fury that
you are your mind's a fucking hurricane just let loose and
live the game true to yourself and your name count your
life not in years count not at all just be here.

Every second of every day becomes surreal the Gods at
play for what are you but part of nature a blade of grass
a fucking tree is no different than you or me just ordered
wondrous energy scratch the surface and you will see
the magic of the mystery a heartbeat like a galaxy keeps
time with your favourite melody as all your desires simply
fade your imagined needs a memory your fears lost on
the morning breeze your mind as one with the glorious
Sun your heart beats louder than a roaring gun your
body shakes your skin's on fire the energies building
higher as the moons of Linium flash past like drops of
rain it makes you wonder why we name every star in
every sky 'cause do they know and do they care a mirror
hanging in the air will show the way if you dare find truth
and beauty everywhere.

Starting now life's a song and do you need tomorrow's burden a day's a day that is enough take some time think about it love yourself and never doubt it 'cause now's as real as life gets no ambitions no regrets no self pity no introspection we're moving to another dimension layer on layer fade away rejoice the dawning of the day behind your eyes starlight flashes a thousand suns turned to ashes a million moons blown to dust the Universe gone supernova a baby screams out for his mother in the whirling madness of a lifetime the clouds explode in glorious sunshine the mirror glows look through as nightime fades away and in your mind the spark rekindled burns strong now and intermingled with your thoughts a music's echo the river's calling softly softly go with the flow the river's wide the river's slow.

Drop the mask of alter-ego the star that once you were and will be holds your place this crazy jigsaw that we call life is now a picture of all you were and all you could be truth is yours it never left you just you were blind and it was see through you were deaf and it was silent you walked alone it walked behind you life is lightning life is thunder life is screaming glorious wonder life is magic life is living your unique one in a billion ask a fish is life worth living yes Hell yes just keep on swimming the current's strong so just go with it the music's loud your heart beats with it this world is yours for the taking the future's yours in the making and in the blinking of an eye you paint the Earth and then the sky and though because you're born you'll die you needn't let life pass you by.

Does a fish believe in water is there life in bricks and
mortar should you bow down to an altar or a man who
wears a collar forgives a sin for just a dollar and says
he speaks for God Himself but knows no more that
what he's told by other men who cannot know you look
through your eyes see things as you do comprehend
what it is to be you and wouldn't know you if they met
you the mirror's there just scratch the surface you do exist
you have a purpose life is learning without ending time
is precious time's for spending in pursuit of Neverland
a billion people hand in hand greet the Sun and on
command the clouds line up and start the chant the day
is here the day is here fuck your worries lose your fears
trust your eyes trust your ears trust your instincts the world
is yours.

Forever fifteen yeah I wish but time moves on for this wee
fish and though I wanna be Peter Pan I know I'm not just
act like I am but perhaps that might just be enough to
keep me smiling with a hold on me brock the world is still
a place of promise with real superheroes just like in the
comics and though everyone I meet will tell me I'm wrong
you can all go and fuck while I sing a hero's song living
doesn't frighten me it never fucking will perhaps my death
smiles back at me but even death can't kill a being made
of energy of energy that's real with each new day I get a
glimpse of what there is to see each grain of truth a grain
of sand on a massive fucking beach where every grain is
beautiful and every grain unique every grain carved with
its name if only we could see.

The world is small the world is shrinking your mind
expands without thinking all is clear all is see through
learning what it means to be you stepping stones to a life
that's different from what you thought was your existence
there is another place in time that looks like this but is
deeper look just look that fucking mirror stares at you and
shows the real world growing now and learning through
you life is just a stream of numbers do the maths you'll
see what's under what you thought was the surface is just
a show a fucking circus walk in doubt walk in pity just
another Walter Mitty close your eyes your heart will teach
you how to walk each day like it's new sparkling clouds
and melting dew tell the story let it fill you dreams reveal
all that is true.

In your hands the future's plastic mould it shape it it's
fantastic the road's uphill but you will make it enjoy the
view and never fake it life's a bitch but ain't it magic spin
the dice to your advantage 'cause when the Kings come
out to play a billion people shout hooray hooray for
Henry hooray for John hooray for every mother's son and
mother's daughter on this Earth who live their lives for all
it's worth and take pleasure in the day the pessimists in
disarray 'cause life is real life's amazing not just hot it's
fucking blazing it's all uphill so run like crazy trust your
feet and don't get lazy don't ever let the bastards tell you
life is shit it has to be so they are blind they are wankers
so run like fuck and be thankful your mind is free of the
anchors of desire of fear of anger.

Run like mad the future's waiting that walking sleep that fucking daydream is fading now and then a moonbeam lights the way through beauty's slipstream to a place where Kings on carpets fly above their castle parapets and Queens with crowns glow with goodness beauty there in abundance you the Earth the Sun the Universe one and the same a set of numbers do the maths your thoughts are thunder your mind's a whirl of random patterns but somehow ordered somehow flattened almost sounds like a billion children rang the biggest bells they could find you are a temple of life itself so run like hellfire stronger now 'cause though it's uphill you'll glimpse the view it makes it worthwhile drink the air eat the sunshine hear the sound of frost at night time.

A billion people clap their hands and sing their way to Neverland can't stop now the wheel's in motion intoxicated with life's potion drunk on air stoned on starlight far from caring if the world is truth or daring young or old still or spinning ask a question there's the answer you're the drummer and the dancer life's a stew but now your cookin running naked but who's lookin rest your head when you're tired don't be ashamed to be desired life's a mess but in beauty's slipstream an ordered labyrinth of day dreams spins a web strong as steel and more complex than an atom brighter than the Sun at high noon with more colours than you could imagine a web in which Mars and Saturn are just like you just ordered matter held together by the same life force that spins the Sun and makes the grass grow.

You've more power than a tornado an earthquake and
ten volcanoes could barely dent the mirror's surface
life's the show not a rehearsal so don't feel like your life
lacks purpose and all you value fucking worthless for
that is sin sin is failure to take your share of this life's
treasure 'cause you're the same as me we're monkeys
nameless sheep faceless donkeys if you look life in the
eye the mirror glows in broad daylight a player gambles
everything loses all and wins again life's a gamble so
keep on betting play the game without forgetting there
are no rules just different settings and each time you
lose you'll learn a lesson it'll make you stronger a better
person but never give up never say enough 'cause when
the game gets going go-getters play rough.

Can you say you're an individual or just a product of
society's treadmill dragging your feet as you leave the
production line packaged stamped conned into thinking
like every other fucker with a cage 'round his mind you'll
never do it so don't even try don't listen to them send in
the sheep shearers it must be true I read it in the papers
the game goes on don't sit on the sidelines waiting for
someone to say it's your turn now's your turn you're
ready and able lunch is served it's on the table so just dig
in and love every mouthful savour the flavour living is so
cool eating drinking walking thinking are all important
the world's still shrinking soon you'll find it fits in your
pocket picture a star-scape your mind's a rocket drop
your ego you don't really need it life is an animal energy
feeds it.

Don't hold back be all you can be bend the fabric of your reality 'cause all it is is fucking atoms quarks and molecules arranged in a pattern all connected all in motion physical matter and emotion one and the same in life's strange potion an incredible tapestry weaving there for men who do not seem to care work all your life and then retire wait to die your past a mire of things you wish that you had done when you were fearless and the world was young thinking there should have been something more another pathway another door different choices different streets different chances and different beats different bridges to different shores where different people wear different clothes and different DJs play different tunes on different decks they echo off the Moon.

A cry went up from Saturn's rings as a billion people danced on wings and though you thought outer space was silent listen closely in the distance there is an echo of a future dance floor where a billion people wearin boots dance hardcore a future city in outer space we travelled at light speed to get to the place nine giant speakers each as big as Earth orbited the dance floor the dancers held their breath the first of many DJs stepped up to the decks and slowly very slowly the floor began to pulse the people getting restless just as the sky lit up a thousand different colours a million fireworks and then as one they screamed come on the DJ let it rip the dance floor took a beating as every dancer kicked their way into oblivion they kicked the floor to bits.

Ah yes Little One your time is coming the pathway's
lit life is loving all around and in a circle energy flows
under the surface waiting there for you to plug in life is a
gamble what are the stakes boot down all the way to Hell
with the brakes top gear full speed straight as an arrow
the road might be long but the path is narrow givin it
socks 'cause what's the alternative standing still is going
backwards there are no keys no secret passwords the
door is open so run like a bastard enjoy all the good stuff
life has to offer 'cause every second is time immortal not
by your watch but in a continuum all things happening
ad-infinium imagine if for just one second you could see
the whole world every person was no more than your
reflection ask the mirror one simple question are you a
hero or a victim.

Do you see a human being immortal unstoppable eyes
bright as sun beam fractured battered but fighting like a
bastard a ball of energy a beautiful being an incredible
machine running at top speed a glorious life a piece of
history an epic story just as it's beginning bet like fuck
and keep on winning gamble the lot on one spin of the
wheel you might not win but at least it's real for those
few seconds while the roulette wheels spinning your mind
is clear your eyes unblinking your ears near deafened
by the rattle of a ball rolling in the opposite direction to
all of the numbers and the one on which is resting every
penny you've ever earned and the same again that you
borrowed from a friend hold your breath hold your nerve
you'll win my son 'cause that's what you deserve.

Life is gold life is silver but life's more precious than these
two put together life in air life in water life in every son
and daughter life in marbles life in seashells life is a
puzzle life is a dictionary life so simple a self contained
mystery life is fierce life is surprising it's all you have so
better get cracking kick ass rampage take no prisoners
all ahead full steam to Hell with the losers bullet straight
towards the Sun every day as important as the last
one for who can say when the time will come to check
out of this skin and try on another one and if you get
a monument to your deeds or a forgotten headstone
covered in weeds you won't really care and it won't really
matter if you were a King or a pauper the worms won't
care 'cause six foot under we're all the same just meat for
the grinder.

Who gives a fuck about the Jones life's no easy ride no
bed of roses life is hard slog life is uphill life takes focus
and strength of will life is a fucker life is a fist fight but at
least you're alive and somehow it feels right and though
you carry the world on your shoulders never look down
'cause your walking a tightrope your back is hurting
your feet are stinging your eyes water and your ears are
ringing your belly's empty your mouth is dry but you
know you'll make it if you try walk with confidence walk
with grace walk like a man who knows his place walk
'cause it's your path walk as you wish to steady now truth
will win through doing your own thing to Hell with the rat
race 'cause if you win it you're still a rat is that all of your
ambition just another fat cat.

A fire breathing Dragon a steel hoofed Unicorn a cigar
smokin cowboy an inter-stellar submarine a view of
the planet from the outer atmosphere a herd of kibous
camels giraffes and fucking kangaroos all look real on
the telly when you're only two and how could you tell
which were real which were fiction you just didn't care it
was all television but not as much fun as the adventure
playground kitchen or the wild wonderland of an
overgrown garden friendly giants everywhere who exist
just to protect you faces smile just 'cause you play and
when you're hungry feed you who carry you when you're
tired who can heal cuts with a kiss and always know the
answers to every crazy question what they said was good
enough though mostly it was nonsense.

As one gets older one's demands from life alter myriad
needs for a body mostly water few men will ever say they
are happy with their lot or look you in the eye and say
all I need is all I've got a roof over your head some food
in your belly some friends to pass the time with and a
coloured fucking telly was all you ever needed when you
were little your needs are still the same my son but your
mind tells you different I want a yacht I want a jet I want
my own island I want a hundred million pounds in gold
and fucking diamonds I want to be the one who makes
the decisions I want the power and the glory sit on my
self made millions in this urban jungle the winners call
the shots around them people bow and scrape and run to
keep their jobs.

And yes he may tell himself now I've fucking made it
but in his heart a shade of doubt asks what do you hold
sacred and all he has achieved will one day be a shadow
a billion years is but a blink in true times endless echo
the Earth itself is just a ball of cooling fucking lava barely
a dot near a tiny sun whose fire is just a fraction of the
power that arises from human interaction because from
where you are everything surrounds you see things with
the eyes of a child true beauty just astounds you if you
were teleported to a far off distant planet the Earth and
Sun would disappear in a sky of coloured fragments
behold The Show and clap your hands as the curtain
rises on all the actors from all the scenes in all their
different guises.

Making money is well and good if you know how to
spend it but never let it blind you to the worth of your
existence a life is worth ten times more than any fucker's
fortune life's about experience not just social ladders if
you think that to live well you need a great big mansion
you're wrong my son you just need a little under-standing
and the ability to appreciate the miracles around you the
world is yours if you want just sign the fucking papers
have you ever met a person who looks like he's on fire
if you do ask him why his life looks that bit brighter
perhaps he sees things that you can't because your path
is winding while his is straight to that place where the
view is almost blinding or maybe he's just realised that
treasure's in the finding.

Shadows and dust Little One have you seen The Circus that starts as this wee planet turns itself away from our Sun's surface track the planets as they move slowly through their orbits compared to space Neptune's so close you could reach and touch it a tapestry of many strings whose background has absorbed it Saturn's rings are faded beams a distant shiny marble Pluto doesn't even count a dot upon a carpet Earth is just a little speck on a desert landscape Mars only a skinny fish a minnow in the ocean Mercury a tiny stone beside the highest mountain Venus seems a drop of water in a twenty mile high fountain Jupiter a single grape in a vineyard one of millions Uranus a bony little ass on a beach of naked billions the Milky Way a hidden gem a diamond in a coal mine.

The greatest show of all plays on with you it's very centre perhaps the Ancients were not so wrong when they placed Earth in the middle the Earth it seems could even be the centre of the Universe but more precise it is yourself who must decide the answer look out not up at the stars as night-time's curtain rises there is no up or down out there just infinite surprises a mystery to it's self whose purpose we can't guess at an enigma wrapped in a sham of chaotic mixed up algebra why is it there what's it for is it on a mission the product of some strategy of billions of decisions or is it just a random mess of whirling bits of matter no order to what it does just chance brings things together whatever it is here's one sure thing it's amazing to behold I stood out there on Linium and watched The Show unfold.

How could I describe to you the view from where I'm
sitting our Universe a ball of string at the mercy of
a kitten one of many pretty things in the adventure
playground kitchen that in itself was enough for endless
heroic missions some of which required the use of all
the kitchen dishes others which involved every blanket
you could muster and half a dozen which kicked off
with two sofas and ten cushions the fridge was fucking
booby trapped well that's what I believed only Ma could
open it and Da in times of need the area around the fire
was mined at every angle otherwise the kitchen was a
domesticated jungle and everything hanging 'round was
used without exception in the manic mighty mayhem of a
little boy's progression from flat on his belly to standing
up to three-hood's life time lessons.

We wonder how the little ones absorb so much so quickly
and marvel as they get the knack of how to spit or whistle
learning the different reactions to each facial expression
the sounds of language the power of tears and using
emotional blackmail to get your Ma to say ok after twenty
times saying no did you ever have to think back then
about your life's direction onward and upward more than
enough to make a day a mission fightin fit and made
of steel eyes like saucers and incredible zeal to learn
everything the world had to offer and take to knowledge
like a duck to butter the world's no different now my son
just a whole lot bigger and a lot more fun to me it seems
we've all just forgotten to take life's knocks like a smack
on the bottom.

Do you think your mind calculates one billion things per second well if it didn't how could you think or even read this sentence your mind's a store of ten times more than you could ever guess at so are you gonna be a player or just another lab rat conditioned into thinking exactly as they told you believing all the horse shit that they fed you at your school you have to be competitive you have to be a winner you have to be top of the class you have to queue for dinner you have to wear this jacket this shirt and fucking tie everything they make you do a cage around your mind you have to play outdoor sports you have to sit and listen to a little man with glasses who spews out information and puts you down if you question him or show imagination.

So what is it that you gain from years of education a piece of paper that simply states you're qualified at something or if you're good a degree that lands you with the right job to spend the next forty years at work and paying taxes take two weeks off in a year and go and get your ass burnt just like you did the year before but in a different country though it might have been a different place the plot's always the same come back and boast to all your friends how life's so good in Spain about the cost of living or the food upon the plane and how it was so much fun and how it never rained and how you wished your holiday never had to end and where you're going next year if you have the money if that's all you're working for then keep on working sonny.

But if you did would you admit that you had a shit time
the plane delayed the food was crap and everything
expensive the attractions all over-priced and the locals
just offensive could you tell all your friends your two
weeks were a washout you got the runs on the first day
and then that night mosquitoes bit your ass so many times
you couldn't even sit down lie in the sun all afternoon and
later in the shower you look at yourself and you'll say
how nice and fucking brown but as you lay asleep that
night your suntan turns to blisters the mosquitoes have
returned to suck upon your blood stream the doctor says
you'll need pills and factor forty sunscreen to top it off
you realise you've now got constipation and in your mind
blame your wife 'cause she chose the destination.

Back to work for fifty weeks but is it really worth it post-
holiday blues sit 'round your head and all you've got is
photos to remind you of how good it felt just fourteen
days of pleasure look at it and realise society is a
prison there's no freedom in democracy just a notion
of free living self-government's a fucking joke it's all
just institutions and freedom to vote simply a way to let
another make decisions so what then of the individual
who can't and won't conform or shape himself to behave
in a way considered norm hail you I do if you are a
genuine free spirit and if you've got the balls to say it's
my life I'll live it true to myself and my name and what
I think's important stuff your fucking shirt and tie your
pension plans and mortgage.

So what say you you wondrous person are you real or just a version of what the people around you wanna see a good little soldier a society wannabe an upstanding citizen a God fearing Christian a productive number of the capitalist system a law abiding nobody in suburban boredom a lone commuter on a train packed with hundreds all docile as cattle ear-tagged and numbered givin your best for the sake of the economy hoping that this time you'll make that deadline gotta do good gotta give the right impression gotta make the boss think you're made for this profession gotta get a pay rise two points above inflation and a good Christmas bonus to buy expensive presents gotta get a pat on the head gotta get promoted gotta have share options 'cause your company's just been floated.

Do you think the job you do is really that important to your life as a human being or could you live without it have you ever thought about a life without those pressures just having enough to survive but rich with life's true treasure we are we think the highest form of organic evolution a thinking talking walking mix of solids and solutions we rule the planet we live on and have done now for ages now it's time to free ourselves from our mental cages put there by our history and re-enforced in stages at the edge of your mind there is a place the bastards couldn't get to a place where the fire that is a man if channelled right can burn through any doubts or fears you had about the worth of your existence after all we are number one we're nature's chosen species.

I've read somewhere that if it wants an elephant can give
up living not exactly kill itself but just switch off all engines
how fortunate that Mother Nature did not give us that
weakness we'd probably have died out long ago 'cause
humans think they're Pygmies given the choice to struggle
on or just lie down and drift off many a caveman might
have thought the former's just not worth it indeed the
latter may look like a more attractive option even today
is there a man who has not thought ah fuck this and
wished he was a babe again sucking his Ma's tits with
every need catered for exactly when you wanted and not
a thought of what lay ahead a life of warmth and comfort
not knowing that a time will come when life's hard work
and bullshit.

Do you think you might survive until you are a hundred
or perhaps even a hundred and ten you can but do
you want to the time we live has increased with each
new generation life expectancy is going up faster than
inflation what ages us is how we think and treat our lives
in stages from puberty to pension hood those fucking
mental cages make us think that at a certain age it's time
to cash your chips in don't listen my son just because
your Da died when he was fifty doesn't mean that you'll
be lucky to make it through to sixty there's no reason
you can't survive twice as long as he did I'd even say he
would be proud of his son's achievement so when the
government says it's time for you to draw the pension
laugh at them and tell them why it's gonna cost a fortune.

I thought me head was in the shed I thought life was a fucker I thought my ass was made of lead I thought my mates were pucker I thought I was a skinny kid my thoughts as loud as thunder I thought that words were silly things I knew that roots grow under ground I knew all maths was numbers I knew which fruits were good to eat and which plants lead to water I knew that one could dance all night I know that death is murder I learned that Paris was in France I learned that grapes made wine I learned that frogs say silly things I learned that life's divine I saw the moons of Linium look just like grapes on vines I saw a man in clouds of mist waiting for his time I watched a boy become a man I watched as night gave way to the million twisting mysteries contained in that one day.

I thought TV was like real life I thought me Ma was lovely I thought that all men spoke the truth and that all bears were cuddly I thought a hero was a man whose deeds got good PR I learned that life has many shades and not just right and wrong I knew the Sun rose in the east I knew that hens lay eggs I knew that rain made you wet and that my blood was red I learned that taste was only one of many magic senses I learned to walk and then to run and finally jump fences I learned that if one wants to dance one has to pay the piper I felt the pain of being born in every cell and fibre I heard my scream they cut the cord a far flung painful memory I found that introspection leads to self doubt and depression but then I felt my heart beat strong and knew I had a mission.

I learned that love is stronger than the rocks this Earth is made of I learned that if he wants a man can live his life in shadow I learned a child is wiser than most people over forty I learned that space is infinite but what that means don't ask me I also know that history is written by the victors and I know fighting for peace is fucking for virginity I know that ordered energy is all we were and will be I know that to himself a man will always be a mystery I feel that truth waits underneath there to be discovered I've seen the mirror in the air my reflection on its surface I've seen an ocean with no shore whose water teems with life I've seen a city of a million beings that's only there in moonlight I once crossed over the threshold of pain but by being born we all might.

I must have been a crazy kid to think the world was fair naive I'd say 'cause I thought each man gets his share silly perhaps when I believed in Santa and the Tooth Fairy but what does one do when you're only two but believe in what they tell you a little later as I grew up they told me I was Catholic that God was real and to be feared and a piece of bread was dead flesh you tricked me once you stupid fucks with your collars and your bullshit and when you made me kneel and pray to a man being executed nails in his hands and in both feet with thorns around his head looking almost slightly bored but very plainly dead gazing down from a cross of wood his sad eyes told me quietly this is wrong my son those stupid fucks made a death cult in my memory.

Honestly Ted it had the mind of a train the body of a bus
and the manners of a camel on acid walked like a horse
swam like a cat drank rum like it's going outa fashion
spoke ten languages not all of them human sang like
a pigeon whose balls are swollen claws like pitchforks
teeth like daggers eighteen eyes ears like a rabbits x-ray
vision skin like a lemon farting poison and spitting venom
eating trees and chewing rocks smashin up cars and
smokin pot goin like a fucker shoutin like thunder and in
its wake destruction and murder animals skinned people
naked buildings flattened nothing was sacred farmers
better lock up your daughters board up the windows and
load all the shotguns it's trigger happy and loves playing
poker wears a cowboy hat and laughs like a joker.

If ya had to hear the bastard singing me ears were
bleeding and me eyes were stinging it was ten feet tall
half covered in feathers wore high heel boots and biker's
leathers it doesn't have a brain that we might speak of
just an on and off switch and a gearbox stuck in top it
doesn't cast a shadow or need oxygen to breathe it can
eat beer bottles and doesn't even bleed it's fuelled on
diesel eats whores for breakfast travels like fire and is
totally reckless has never been photographed or caught
on camera snorts shed loads of coke only dances to
gabba it could hide behind the telly or under the bed
had a six foot wig and eyes blood red it could fly like a
chopper and sting like a bullet but honest ta God I think
the wig was a mullet it doesn't have a colour you could
mention and appears at will in any dimension.

It had tits like turnips all over its body drives a Renault
Clio or sometimes an Audi it doesn't have a conscience
or know the meaning of pain it doesn't need sleep
stays dry in the rain it can blend itself into any given
background a localised riot that doesn't make a sound if
it doesn't want to but when it does it sounds even better
than death from above it tore through hedges left scrap
of fences chewed brick walls to their foundations it can
run faster than a formula one car and if it wants jump
fifty feet in the air it can piss pure acid and shit high
explosives it's bullet proof and breathes fire out its nostrils
it could nail you to the spot with just one glance it loves
reading Shakespeare and soppy romance it answers
to the name of Benny I saw the fucker once is south
Kilkenny.

It had fourteen tails and fifteen arses it eats whole cows
barely leaves a carcass it can breathe underwater survive
in outer space its been around longer than the entire
human race people think he's a myth or maybe a legend
but it's uglier than anything we imagine its got rings on
its fingers and bells on its toes tattoos on its balls and a
bar through its nose God help if you ever meet that fucker
don't bother trying to run just accept it you're supper if
you're lucky it will eat you there and then but if not it
might take you back to its den where perhaps it'll stick a
skewer up your arse or stew you slowly with spuds and
carrots it might skin you alive and dip you in sugar or
maybe even mash you up and use you as butter 'cause if
there is one thing he loves most is a mashed up human
spread evenly on toast.

An Urban Indiana Jones once told me what he lived for
he said that to be real this life has to be adventure in his
eyes there was a look I could only call inspiring his skin
as tight as a drum his mouth wide and smiling I couldn't
guess how old he was I didn't think to ask him but I could
tell from his face he knew of life's true meaning and when
he spoke his words were few but rang with quiet wisdom
I don't care who you are he said as long as you've got a
dream to him all people were the same he didn't care for
titles he walked as tall as any man and revelled in life's
battles I have stood in the eye of the storm he said and
saw the world spin round me there is a place somewhere
he said where truth and beauty merge a place where all
men's thoughts and dreams seamlessly converge.

There will be times in this life one meets a true believer
but don't ask what he believes and he won't ask you
either for every person on this Earth there is a path quite
different but each one has its own rewards and each its
own strange blue-print all have worthy noble tasks and
all of great importance all will bring a man to ask is this
life really worth it all will give a chance to be a hero or
a victim if you're lucky you are born with arms two legs
and vision the gift of sight is worth more than a hundred
thousand million if you can walk then fucking run 'cause
it's boring in the slow lane surround yourself with images
from your very own hall of fame here today gone
tomorrow life's fortunes can be fickle so play to win and
bet on yourself right down to your last nickel.

An Urban Indiana Jones is quite a strange companion
if he had been one of the Three Musketeers he would
have been D'Artagnan a modern day hero in a world
filled with victims a friendly wolf among the flock a giant
among pygmies he had his own moral code his own set
of values he always did things his own way and never
thought of failure he never stayed anywhere too long his
home was where his boots were he only worked to make
a buck and only when he had to for a man who had
done so much he was modest almost humble if living has
taught me aught he said it's that life's a fucking gamble
so bet on yourself and play to win you know you can
you fucker bet your ass and hang on tight the wheels just
started spinning you can choose to win or lose it's time
you started winning.

To an outside observer his behaviour would often verge
on the outrageous but if they knew what drove the man
they'd find his manner contagious he really lived for the
love of the game he knew the prize was worth it wherever
he travelled he did so by land or boat if there was water
there's beauty in every view he said as his eyes glossed
over there's colour in every scene he said as his voice
fell to whisper there's gold in every stream he said if you
know how to find it there's music in every sound he said
if you only care to listen a plant's a living thing he said
there's more than gold that glistens in that stream where
a human being's life is quietly mirrored beneath the
waves it's like liquid silk a million coloured stones and
day-glo fish.

The ancient philosophers and modern day scholars all have something in common they all have the same vocation in life that is the pursuit of knowledge the greatest thinkers of all time have not been men of letters but rather have been simple men who simply honed their senses one of humanity's greatest gifts is the power of perception to solve a problem and find the answer regardless of the question do you think that Einstein's brain was made of something different than yours or mine if you've got a mind you're half way to being a genius I spoke before of the power of thought and no I was not kidding we each are born with an accumulated store of knowledge from our parents trace the line back through time ten thousand lifetimes' lessons.

As a species we keep advancing despite the wars and chaos as we hand the future to our kids we can't let the past betray us think back to when we lived in caves as simple hunter gatherers biologically we're much the same but we've built on our ancestor's progress in Afghanistan the Taliban blew up a statue of Buddha but what did that prove except that those fools have got their heads up their asses they said at the time they did it because the statue offended Allah but if there is a God and his name is Allah do you think he has time to hate statues the things that we've done then pinned blame on the Gods whose laws we claim to follow a thousand wars ten million deaths simply defy all logic you don't believe in what I believe in so it's my God given right to kill you.

The Ancient Egyptians the Greeks and the Romans all had many Gods the modern day Christians in fact most religions have narrowed it down to just one but what does it matter if you worship a planet an animal or just an idea a well known church has killed thousands of people in the name of a man from Judea but can the Pope say God wants it this way let's swap our Bibles for guns as a species we hate to admit we are a vicious predator so now we distance ourselves from the killing by doing it in an abattoir we eat the flesh of our fellow beasts we kill them in their millions use the leftovers to make into burgers and wear clothes made from animal skins a man is a killer that is his nature and so it always has been a man will bring murder onto his brother and think that by praying he's clean.

So what have we learnt from the mistakes of the past I fear sometimes very little as people we've killed far more people than famine drought and disease atom bombs mustard gas napalm and lead bullets only exist 'cause we want them to and all we have used in buckets the horror of war the human cost could never be calculated but perhaps we're changing and starting to think that war is simply outdated there are far better ways to communicate and to get the things we need can it be right when politicians are wrong that innocent men have to bleed can it be right that a single man can visit death on millions can it be right that death is doled out by stupid politicians with the stroke of a pen it could be life or death to entire populations.

So if it's money that makes you happy then good on you my son but trust me it will take more than a thousand if you really wanna have fun I'd say it would take at least a million to get the party going but to be honest I can't really say 'cause I don't have much more than a street bum well yes I do have a place that's my home and a circle of magical friends there's Cowboy and Pockets and Sham and Phil and a wee skinny DJ called Ben each of these guys have got nerves made of steel and worth more than their weight in diamonds or gold or fucking platinum or any jewel you could mention each of them a shooting star a walking supernova so if it's living that keeps you ticking then watch as these guys take over kickin ass and walkin tall a million dollar smile and havin a ball.

If you think life's a trip and buzz drugs are hip then come on join the party somewhere right now those big beats are playing and thousands of people are dancing if life is a bitch then treat it like one if life is a ride then fucking jump on if life is pure music who's writing the song life is adventure just ask Cowboy John life is a movie disguised as a play life is a daydream lived in one day life is a journey whose pathways are endless with all of its signposts in a different language life is experience living itself life is a gamble the future's not set life is a question turned inside out the mirror reflecting shadows of doubt that just fade away and sometimes the answers appear out of nowhere unasked for but landing right at your feet just when you needed just within reach.

Try to imagine your life in slow motion seen from above
we're just fish in an ocean of concrete and bricks and
urban commotion although we wear clothes and all think
we're different we follow the herd and live by its instinct
we eat the same food and drink the same water and all
of us somebody's son or their daughter most of us carry
emotional baggage moral dilemmas and sentimental
luggage most of us wish our lives had real substance a
little bit more than just plain existence most of us wish that
someday we'll marry our perfect partner and simply be
happy such things are noble such things are worthwhile
such things will push you that one extra mile but such
things should not be the be-all and end-all there's always
more questions more mysteries to solve.

Back in the sixties they put men on the Moon I wasn't
around just that they told me in school and why did they
bother why all that effort to prove a point or to make
our lives better a small step for man a giant leap for
mankind bring back a few rocks leave footprints behind
our first baby steps into the great and unknown our first
space conquest we've conquered the Moon and what
did it prove except that we could and made heroes of
men in funny white suits and what of the men who first
climbed Mount Everest was it just for the view or to prove
they're the best these are the lengths of human endeavour
these are the benchmarks by which we will measure our
species' progression from caveman to spaceman then
whatever comes after.

I once knew a guy we called him the Ninja simply
because his hair was bright ginger his eyes were like
silver his skin pale as death but the man had more life
than most men I've met he was always the one leading
the charge and left behind him chaos and carnage he
was six foot two and thin as a bean pole a crystal mind a
heart made of pure gold he loved to go fishing as much
as go drinking and often would just sit quietly thinking
about beauty in form or brand new religions he said
man's only flaw was the possession of ego and when
he got going his mind worked in free-fall and when he
spoke everyone listened not 'cause they had to his stories
were brilliant he could conjure a picture with his hands in
the air we listened enchanted the Ninja laid bare.

He spoke from the heart or else not at all his passion for
living inspired us all he thought he was crazy most of the
time and I would agree he's as crazy as I am he lived for
excitement the thrill of the chase a shining example to our
pitiful race I'll live while I'm breathing that's what he said
I'll drink 'cause I want to and sleep when I'm dead to
him being drunk was like you being sober to him being
spaced out was just ticking over don't believe what they
tell you was one of his mottos never give up or take no for
an answer his favourite people were those most extreme
his favourite pastime was drinking with them I live in a
moment that's what he said as he keeled over backward
his eyes bloodshot red and as he lay there down on the
floor he cursed like a gypsy and swore like a whore.

Eight thirty a.m. the Ninja got started by half past four
he'd drunk fourteen bars dry gob-shites he howled as
we dragged him away a pox on your sandwiches he
screamed at the barmaid never surrender echoed through
town find me a pub the day is but young whose round
is it anyway as he wrestled a bar stool the drinks are on
me as he attempted to play pool all aboard boys as he
hijacked a tractor and drove it straight through the wall of
the next bar drunk I'm not drunk ya bunch of wee fuckers
I'll show ya what drunk means we're slammin Tequilas
snortin vodka shootin gin skullin brandy get the rounds
in to Hell or to Connaught there's no place for women
drinkin's a man's work home for the afters falling down
drunk then gettin up plastered.

One foot in the grave one on the wagon a six pack on
one arm on the other a flagon I think best when drunk he
said with conviction my mind only works well when totally
pickled the man had the brain of a great mathematician
and though truly insane could still out-think Nietzsche he
saw the world sideways or backwards or slanted life is
a gamble so just take your chances opportunity knocks
only one time so follow your heart and go spend your
time 'cause life is really a spiritual adventure in a physical
body the rest is a side-show you have to live life in total
excess keep pushing your body and don't let it rest and
so you bring honour to the name of your Fathers your
blood is theirs too your eyes are their windows your path
follows theirs their feelings your senses.

I've always had a fixation with fisting not that I've tried
it just wishful thinking the executive fist the casual fist
the long distance fist the free style fist the two minute
fist the hard core fist the open plan fist the full on fist
the therapeutic fist the digital fist the American fist the
old fashioned fist the double fist the hop skip and fist
the kangaroo fist the middle weight fist the marathon
fist the right wing fist the auto fist the knee length fist the
holy fist the faggots fist the straight fist the ambidextrous
fist the mother of all fists the bare knuckle fist the black
eyed fist the vegetarian fist the royal fist the group fist the
fantasy fist the ghost fist the runaway fist the official fist
the smoking hot fist way past your wrist so get out the
marigolds and the butter think of England and fist the
fucker.

Now well may you think I'm a bit of a sicko that's just the
beginning I'd fist a hippo I'd fist a donkey a goose or a
whale it might be a pinch but I'd fist a quail I'd fist fuck
a corpse a nun or a horse I'd fist whole chickens without
remorse I'd fist fuck a phone box a telly a sheep fisting's
emotional fisting is deep I'd say when I'm dreaming I
fist in my sleep fisting is personal a true communication
a relaxing pastime perhaps a vocation and if you're the
fister or the fistee fist fuck with pleasure fist fuck with glee
sometimes I wish there was a fisting Olympics where the
worlds greatest fisters would meet and set records I heard
this once but it's only a rumour that fisting was practised
by Stalin and Hitler fist in the morning fist in the night
fisting is top notch fisting's all right.

And yes so you see it's a bit of an obsession fisting with style fisting with passion grant me a wish I'd fist the whole race it could make your day put a smile on your face some people might think that fisting is dirty then go fist yourself I tell you it's worth it so if you've got a moral dilemma don't sit on the fence go get an enema there's nothing better to clear your mind than a good friendly fist up your behind if you're a gent or if you're a lady don't be afraid just grin and bear it fisting could be a national pastime with teams and divisions and chants from the crowd fisting on telly or on pay per view with a panel of experts and on-line reviews fisting in public or four day events a summer school or special weekends so if you think that life is too serious a simple cure a fist up your arse.

Fisting in private fisting in tandem fisting as art fisting at random a fisting museum a fisting fucking bible a fisting top ten a fisting revival fist and enjoy fist and reveal your inner self to a fist hard as steel why not have a fisting night school or fisting clubs with members and rules fist in the bath fist in the shower fist on your lawn fist for an hour at a time and then swap over the fister and fistee just taking turns fisting as yoga fisting as Ti-Chi fist fuck your boss or fist an employee fisting animals or fisting furniture fisting machines it's true human nature to explore those things considered taboo and fisting is one of them that is for sure the joy of a sphincter the feel of a colon start it off slowly you just can't go wrong there's nothing better to ease the day's boredom than a friendly fist halfway up your bum.

I said to the boys I want to catch Benny but not to kill him that fat fuck owes me money I knew it would take a twenty strong posse a couple of tractors six nets and some horses so who could I call well first all the Cowboys the Ninja and Sham and maybe a DJ so what was the plan well first we must find him we need some bait how 'bout a virgin finding a virgin is next to impossible the Ninja suggested we use a gay Eskimo we'll have to steal him or trick him to help us they're a difficult bunch these fucking gay Eskimos how 'bout we find one asleep in his igloo and tunnel around it until we can lift it we're going to need a refrigerated lorry we'll nick one from Iceland those bastards have plenty so off they went to get the gay Eskimo and leave him out somewhere till Benny showed up.

The Ninja and Sham and five of the Cowboys went to Alaska to catch us an Eskimo the rest of the Cowboys me and the DJ went to a place we knew Benny would be a small patch of woodland just outside Dublin where Benny hung out when he was hungry we dug three big pits surrounded by trenches hung nets from the trees and built up defences three weeks later the boys had returned with not one but two Eskimos in the back of the truck the pits and trenches we'd covered with branches spread over with leaves rubbish and some grass in the middle we put the first of the igloos it was starting to melt but what could we do the other we kept in the back of the truck then covered ourselves in moss leaves and muck the trap was set we were all ready just had to sit tight waiting for Benny.

46

The DJ had set up and was blasting out gabba from a burger van he'd stolen in Cabra if Benny heard it we knew he'd come running then hopefully sniff out the bait in the igloo and while he was eating or shagging the Eskimo we'd jump from the trenches and let all the nets go so then trying to wrestle his way out of the nets we were sure he'd fall into one of the pits and then we'd have him easy as pie with the only cost one Eskimo's life then like a flash Benny appeared and started dancing over the trees and then he stopped he'd spotted the igloo and said to himself I smell a gay Eskimo he went straight for it and jumped on the roof and tore at the ice blocks with his steel plated hoofs I thought I could hear the Eskimo screaming the poor little bastard thought he was dreaming.

It was all too easy then guess what happened Benny looked up and in surprise farted all we could do was run like the clappers but a wee bit too slow Benny had seen us in a whirlwind of arses he ran at the Ninja but lucky for us the Ninja was plastered come on ya fat fucker as he ran like a bastard Benny charged at him and then just in time a Cowboy had managed to climb up a tree and screamed Benny ya fat fuck come and get me as Benny turned to mangle the Cowboy Sham jumped in and sliced off his ball bag even the hill shook at the scream a split second later he had disappeared and all that was left was two tattooed testicles a smell worse than shite and a terrified Eskimo things had got messy but at least we had tried Benny was wounded we'd chopped off his pride.

A toast to you a merry crew of misfits and strange beings although to yourselves you may seem quite normal to me you are amazing a person's face carries a trace of everything he's been through experience changes you that's how you grow living changing learning your skin remembers everything you are a stream of numbers in constant flux in endless maths that's why we're all so different a pair of twins who look the same are very different people with different dreams and different schemes and very different feelings you realise you are the only one who sees the world as you do no one else can understand and would you really want them to so treat life as a game of chess be a player or a pawn treat life like monopoly and when it's time to move move on.

What if you were handed the choice of what to come back as next time would you come back as you again and give it another try would you do things differently would you make the same mistakes would you live life at top speed or would you use the brakes would you ask to look the same or would you want to be taller or better looking a different colour a different sex or smaller or perhaps you may have learned by then that none of these things matter a body is simply a carved machine in which you chose to travel the machine that you now occupy is entirely at your disposal although it needs certain things it's just for rock and rollin so greet the day with a smile on your face and trust your instincts always greet the day with cold steel eyes a hard-on and a war cry.

Nothing's as sensational as living pure sensation
nothing's quite as wonderful as the stream of our creation
nothing's as amazing as your own imagination nothing's
quite as real as when your first scream hits your ears
nothing can prepare you for the next one hundred years
no one can decide for you which path you should be
taking no one else can make you see you're history in
the making there's only you and this bit's true you are a
one man band as well you are the audience the stadium
the stand if your hero came to you and said son I have
a mission it's just for you and no one else can bring it to
fruition would you accept and think you're blessed and
tackle it head on would you accept and know you're right
though a million said you're wrong.

Have you the balls to say to all it's my trip and I'm trippin
have you the heart to face your death smile and go out
kicking have you the mind to understand this stream that
you're a part of have you eyes to see straight through the
walls we have created are you the kind to feel life's real
and never have to fake it have you ever had a dream so
real you knew there's more to life than racing rats to be
fat cats and saving for your funeral has there ever been a
moment when the jigsaw came together for just a second
but just enough for you to catch a glimpse of what could
be if we learned to live and grow together are you proud
to be a man a woman or whatever do you love yourself
for what you are if you do you're clever and if you're
wise you'll understand that life itself is treasure.

A humble ego-maniac if such a man existed looked out from his mountain top and saw the world was twisted what is this why do these men run from their own shadows what's going on when human beings can't see past their noses surrounded each day by miracles but don't believe in magic greet a day as an ordeal it's worse than sad it's tragic who is this God that they call wealth I've never met the fucker a hundred men own half the world while a billion others suffer if capitalism is man's true religion and making money worship a million people hang on every word of Bill Gates the prophet and yes it's true I am too a part of this strange system that judges men not by their hearts but by how much they make for a living I pity fools I don't despise strength comes of forgiving.

This humble ego-maniac was walking through the City and on all sides he saw the signs of modern urban living men in suits with stern expressions the world upon their shoulders cold stone buildings with blacked out windows to shield us from their purpose if you don't wear a shirt and tie you cannot join the club and if you're not prepared to lie you might not make a buck tell your boss he's wonderful and his ideas genius keep your mouth shut when he's wrong or you'll end up on the dole queue sit at your desk every day and tell yourself it's worth it and think it's great at the years end 'cause the company's still in profit but think on this while you sit each day you're getting older thirty's gone here comes forty and to your kids some random stranger.

Time and tide wait for no man no matter who he is look
at yourself in the mirror be honest what do you see is
the person looking back a hero or a victim is the person
staring out a good man or a villain add it up is that
man a loser or a winner don't worry about the past my
son 'cause once we all were sinners and can you really
comprehend the value of your freedom look at your
hands and your feet your body's not a prison make a list
of just ten things you've always wished you'd done then
get cracking and make it happen the clock is ticking son
are you the kind who always thinks and worries about the
future that is just plain silliness use your eyes they'll teach
you what you are and then why look at the sky at night
time somewhere out there shines a star and it's got your
name on.

Perhaps one day you will decide to reassess your values
perhaps one day you will decide that truth is all that
matters perhaps one day you will wake up just before the
sunrise and as you watch the day begin through your
sleepy eyes the beauty of the mystery hits you like a tide
and if you're lucky you just might feel a part of something
greater more than merely just a man far bigger than your
ego far deeper than the deepest thing our little minds can
fathom far too big to have a name too old to have an
age but part of you just out of reach beyond your mental
cage and if on that any day your humanity strikes home
then thank the Gods of Ancient Greece of Egypt and of
Rome what happens to the Ancient Gods when we forget
their names they just kick back and smoke some dope till
man needs them again.

I couldn't see the rookery for the fucking trees I couldn't
see the honey with all those fucking bees I couldn't see
the broccoli for the fucking carrots I couldn't see the
turkeys with all those bastard parrots I couldn't see past
my nose until my eyes were opened I couldn't see a single
thing my head was up my rectum there was a time my
eyes glanced down on seeing their reflection and I think
I was ashamed just to have an erection I didn't know I
was a giant in a midgets body I didn't know that half the
world is off it's fucking trolley I didn't know that my mind
was in fact a prison I didn't know that underneath the
surface of the jigsaw the colours that we think exist blend
into a black hole where time itself is meaningless and
past and future see-saw.

I couldn't see the mirror hanging in the air I couldn't see
the mystery I didn't even care I couldn't hear the music the
drum beat of the world I couldn't see the Ancient Ones as
they moved among us I thought the world was black and
white and people were bald monkeys there was a time
I didn't know the value of a life a self obsessed mental
dwarf whose daily tasks were strife I didn't know the
world was round and made of different countries I didn't
know my blood was red till I cut myself and seen it I never
knew that simple truth could bring a man to tears I didn't
know that butterflies had once been caterpillars I didn't
know that to make an omelette one had to break some
eggs or how a tiny millipede can have ten thousand legs.

I didn't know that to be alive one has to face one's death
or why a man who's very old wastes time on regret I
didn't know where I came from although I knew my
Mother I did not know that beneath their skin all men are
my brothers to take a life is to kill yourself to take your
own is worse life's the greatest gift you have life is not
a curse I did not know that if one tried one could really
make a difference not just to one's own life but perhaps
a million peoples' I've seen the world I thought was real
melt away like frost and in the spinning tapestry I saw I
too was lost but that was then and this is now my feet are
on the ground and though my eyes have seen my death
my grip on life is sound in every day while I walk I learn I
grow I love and the person I became fits me like a glove.

Overhead a rainbow glows perhaps for just a minute and
at its end a crock of gold if only you could find it chasing
rainbows that's my life I know I'll never catch one but
life's a trip and this is mine a body built for fun think of
how many times your face smiles in a day if it is any less
than one thousand your face will soon show age never
mind your wrinkle creams your hair dye and your facials
simple fun keeps you young as long as you maintain it
the fountain of youth does exist whether you believe it
and miracles are as real as bicycles or peanuts Cowboy
John told me once that all our trials are valid and though
he is a man on fire his eyes are cool as salad and Pockets
too he knows what's cool dance clubs buzz drugs fashion
take the world by the scruff of its neck and fist it with a
passion.

Fear of the world and loathing of the self is detrimental to
one's mind and dangerous for one's health read between
the lines my son you'll see your life's true meaning a
man can travel the entire world and still not learn a
thing the Buddha mind is a blank page without thought
or preconception the mirror's hanging in the air admire
your own reflection how did we know that sand made
glass till some fucker tried it your mind is just the same
my son true beauty lies behind it the matter of which you
are made is as old as time itself just changing form and
being born always changing shape consciousness is just
a bluff your body knows the answer the world is yours
just become the drummer and the dancer the world is
yours the Force is real more real than you imagine.

They told me I was scarred for life they told me I was
bleeding they filled my head with so much shit my poor
wee mind was reeling and though my eyes saw the lies
I never thought to question those people talking out their
holes though they spoke with conviction pretending that
they knew the truth but in fact were only guessing I am
in fact quite surprised my mind survived the onslaught
of gibberish and verbal shit and uninspired thought
how dare they try to mould me into a mental cage be a
carbon copy of stupid men whose mistakes have scarred
their age and whose follies led us to the horror that is war
over forty million dead for who for what what for choose
your leaders carefully ask what is their motive give men
power to abuse is that why you voted.

Even nowadays it gets tricky if you mention Adolph Hitler
an organised man and a bit of a thinker who set himself
a goal and jumped in head and shoulders he might have
been insane but was a feisty wee fucker and people often
overlook a decorated soldier he simply was a product of
the world that he grew up in and also one must not forget
the writings of that Englishman let history be history
the final war is over there will never be a World War
Three we've got too much to live for and do we really
understand the nature of the primate for that is firstly
what we are a naked fucking ape made to hunt made
to kill to savage and to rape our physical form is animal
though we use the pre-fix human we still all have to eat
and shit and kneel for our communion.

Forget about the past at last the future is our baby
revenge for wrongs done in the past can only lead us
backward the planet is a small place now and brothers
we must share it and care for every living thing before
it's just too late the way in which we live now cannot be
sustained must we murder every tree till only dust remains
in the name of progress we wage war on nature but
what harm has nature done us when burning fields and
poisoned seas are all that we have left we ourselves must
take the blame for Mother Nature's death but wait my
son it's not too late we still can turn the tables if we can
put men on the Moon then surely within reason we can
fix the harm we've done bring on the healing season this
planet is not ours you see this planet is our children's.

Ah yes it had been an interesting day we hadn't caught
Benny he'd just got away but now we had a bargaining
chip we had Benny's balls though not his dick I knew that
sometime Benny would come back he needed his balls
if only to spank so now we were faced with a bit of a
problem on Benny's return we had somehow to trap him
no easy task as we'd already learned we were sure he
was pissed off angry as Hell 'cause how would you feel if
when out for your lunch some little fucker sliced off your
nuts a little bit peeved that's understatement rip roaring
livid out of your head we'd frightened the bastard that
was a first he thought he was hard as next time would be
worse we'd dazzle the bastard once he appeared then
spray him with slurry and call him a queer.

We all agreed a brilliant idea the Ninja was fuck eyed
but still he was thinking all we would need was a bag of
explosives a sixty foot pit to Hell with the Eskimos Benny's
balls were the size of a small car weighed over a ton and
covered with kevlar I knew from the last time that Benny
was fast I also knew we'd get just one chance we found
a deep well and dropped Benny's balls in we knew he'd
come back just a matter of when a Cowboy went off to
buy shed loads of dynamite we set up camp and waited
for three nights then Benny appeared what a surprise it
was the same Benny but dressed in disguise he looked
like a dump truck covered in handbags with dreadlocks
and earrings and a flag out his main ass he looked down
the well and sniffed at the air and said to himself I think
the coast's clear.

How could we have known the bastard was trippin he'd eaten more acid than a commune of hippies a clever trick to keep his mind sharp now he could sense us and see in the dark well we were hidden but not well enough Benny's dilemma which one to kill first then like a flash he went straight for Pockets I ran to the well with a bag of explosives Benny ya bastard if you touch my mate I'll blow your balls into a million bits he stopped on the spot and then turned to face me slowly he walked to where I was standing I said please Benny lets do this like gentlemen in his wee girlie voice he said what do you want simple I said you owe me a debt I don't want to hurt you but I will if you make me I'm a nice guy but a bitch when I'm angry.

You ya wee fucker I know you from somewhere yes I said I beat you at poker you wouldn't pay up then and got in a huff that was ten years ago but I don't give up Benny knew I had the advantage ok he said and reached for his handbags how much was it I can't remember I can I said it was three hundred thousand as he was counting out all the money I shouted the boys to make a run for it now then Benny get down the well collect your balls and go back to Hell I knew for a second he couldn't decide which he valued more his balls or his pride he could have killed me there on the spot but no matter how fast the bag would have dropped then at last he admitted defeat smiled and winked at me then spat at my feet as the last of his tails dropped out of sight I laughed to myself then ran for my life.

The greatest man on Earth said boys it's time for the
breakfast pint as he spoke those words his skin gained
colour and his eyes sparked with delight down the stairs
like the clappers front door swinging off its hinges sharp
right-hander into Joyce's above a canopy of whisky
voices I heard Riley shoutin Jesus Mary and Holy St
Joseph this man needs a pint a giant of a man big as a
bear with a distinguished beard and long flowing hair he
laughed like a truck and fought like a tiger drank like a
fish and never ever tired of his incredible life as a party
for hire eleven fifteen with five pints down Riley said boys
let's hit the town there's work to be done and plenty of
it the day is young but time is wastin raise your glasses
we're celebrating the fact we're alive drink to creation.

He always stood while he was drinkin keeps the blood
flowing keeps the mind thinkin a one man storm in
walking defiance of doctors advice and medical science
he always made an entrance when he hit a pub but it's
hard not to when you're built like a bus but beneath the
exterior of this walking mountain lay a heart of gold and
a mind like a fountain he could lecture on history modern
or ancient always spoke softly when he made a statement
he could debate quantum theory with any educated
fucker could recite epic poems at the drop of a hat
converse in Latin explain chaos math and all the while
his eyes still sparkled and his teeth shone brightly as he
laughed at the youngsters simply 'cause they played and
already knew the answers.

He told me once he was a time millionaire I didn't
understand but now the truth is there I remember his
words they're carved in my mind the most amazing man
I was lucky to find a man in a million but more than just
this a living legend on that island's west coast whose
name will be spoken long after he's gone they'll speak
his name in whispers and write many songs they'll build
a statue of him in the middle of the town and on Sunday
afternoons the people gather round and hear tales of
Brendan Riley a King without a crown a man without a
penny or a care in the world a man who lived life on the
edge a mind like a sword time is more than precious time
is all you've got don't ever hang your head feeling sorry
for your lot kick back enjoy the view drink some beer and
smoke some pot.

If he'd had any money they'd have called him eccentric
but since he was broke they just classed him a lunatic
and this he didn't mind he laughed when he heard it but
that was his reaction to most of this life's bullshit ego is
for fools the truth is in your hands your smile is worth a
fortune your world at your command raise your glass and
drink up or lunch will be upon us toast your health with a
dram of Scotch and wash it down with Guinness saddle
up the bicycles we're headin for the hills pedalling fast
out west of town and come back by the east thirty pubs
already done it's now late afternoon standing sober as
a judge Riley's on the town eight hours to go till closing
time lads don't lag behind we are men we are strong
we'll drink until we're blind.

My ego was fist fucked by my mojo the world that I had
thought was real was really made of lego on a heavy
head fuck acid trip my brain began to pogo and as
it turned inside out the fool that once I was let go O
woe is me I used to think that life was really complex I
remembered it was simpler when just sucking a pair of
tits at that age perfection reigned everything was sorted a
place to sleep food to eat and toys there if I wanted each
day held new experience each day a new beginning
each day for me was a waking dream without fear
or rules or limits the King of all he could survey in the
adventure playground kitchen long before I knew a door
was something you could walk through the world at hand
was a kitchen floor and soft toys you could talk to.

I remember Sesame Street such simple propaganda my
first wrist watch my first pocket camera and when the telly
had only one channel I remember when a computer was
a machine in science fiction and a cartoon guy called
Flash Gordon kicked ass on television the ultimate hero
I suppose for a time then joined a list of many whose
adventures all inspired a wee man in Kilkenny who never
got tired of jumping around and smiled most of the time
who never thought of giving up just simply kept on trying
another jump another path another skill to find all were
part of growing up in half wild countryside an all round
magic Kingdom stories came to life the world was such
a simple place when this man was a child not so now so
much to do I miss that life sometimes.

There's bats in the trees run boys like fuck attacked twice
by bees then knee deep in muck back for me wellies then
tore me jeans fell head first into nettles and ass first in a
stream back at the house completely knackered one wellie
missing shirt and jeans in fucking tatters but grinning like
a cat 'cause I was home in time for supper and though I
was a hardy kid my Ma had convinced me that bats can
stick in your head and suck blood if they want to absolute
rubbish but still more than enough to get a wee man
home for supper looking filthy scratched and rough then
after being washed and fed looking like a million bucks
getting drowsy dopey drifting sleepy but trying to stay up
then coloured soft adventure dreams I hated waking up.

It was crazy being eleven getting taller by the day but
it's strange I don't remember growing up by every stage
I was eager to be tall and be a man like Da someday a
stringy little monkey climbing trees and playing games
as wildly energetic as a horse you cannot tame mostly
made of rubber and enjoying local fame as a fearsome
little fucker in my school and to my mates ever the one
up for fun and always stayed out late I used to build
bicycles and race carts in Da's shed I could make a bow
and arrows and fishing weights from stolen lead we used
to catch rabbits with just some sticks and a dog and I
remember we had ducks I used to feed them baby frogs a
mini Indiana Jones who had a bike and not a horse who
never stopped to doubt himself and never once got lost.

Sit quietly round the fire now boys I'll tell you 'bout a man who lived his life in top gear and never had a plan for him things seemed to work out right pick the place name the time he never was a greedy man liked his food and loved his wine he never asked the Gods for much and took only his share he never pushed his luck too far and was constantly aware of the needs of those around him always first to care he had true simple goals in life to share his many blessings respect for all living things and learning through life's lessons integrity that's the key from this the rest will follow he really was a humble man and shy in many ways he never talked about himself and never could take praise he never cared for vanity and never showed his age.

They said that he could heal a man just by looking at him but this was not magic son he simply shared their burden he never could sit quietly and watch a brother suffer he always stood up for the weak no matter what their plight even the sound of the birds could make the fucker smile to watch kids play would make his day he dressed in simple style a travelling man who was at home in any place or situation he knew so much but only spoke when asked his opinion he said his name was Aftermath I never understood it he said that if a man's to live he can't pretend he's stupid he also said that he believed in everything and nothing I asked him what the fuck that meant he said everything and nothing so then I asked him how a man like him can sometimes talk pure nonsense.

I've seen spirits I've seen ghosts I've seen faces in the walls I've seen an Angel stormin livin life with tits no nuts but balls I've seen animals who could talk I've seen squirrels playing tennis I've seen men achieve their dreams then die for lack of challenge I've seen men walk through fire and come out not even singed I've seen even stranger things hidden in the Ether I've seen things that made me scream I've heard the futures' echo I've seen things that normal men would probably call real magic I've seen lead turned to gold I've seen fortunes won and lost I've seen men gamble all and never count the cost I've seen the moons of Linium glistening with frost but all of these no stranger that the shock of being born to find myself alive on Earth I screamed they cut the cord.

And so I sit quietly and smile as lady luck plays the odds for human beings who live to eat and fuck I asked my good friend Aftermath what is life about he said son I cannot tell you that the fun is finding out but behind that fucker's cheeky grin I saw a real compassion then he said the pursuit of dreams will always be in fashion it doesn't matter what you do just do so with a passion it doesn't matter who you are we've all the same potential don't look back don't look down your hopes and dreams essential there may be times when you feel you just can't cut the mustard but don't worry don't give up grit your teeth fight like a bastard and when you go to sleep at night rest easy and be grateful for there are people on this Earth who die though they are faithful.

They say the road to failure is paved with good intention
when I say they I mean he that mad wee fucker Fen Lon
what does he mean I asked myself it's too clear to be a
riddle success and failure on each side free will in the
middle left or right can you trust the signposts made
by others no I say trust yourself your path is not your
brothers and if it rains well never mind it's only going to
wet you and if it snows then make snowballs and throw
them at the snowmen and then at night rest and sleep
'cause sleep's a journey too and every mile a drifting
dream with friends who've never met you enjoy the days
when it's uphill 'cause these just make you stronger free
will is yours evermore but freedom is a burden because
every choice you make casts you the hero or the victim.

Can't rain all the time there'll always be good food and
wine and if you need to unwind then kick back enjoy the
ride a drop of rain the ocean tide one and the same just
separated by a natural process nature created everything
in seasons everything in sync everything in cycles
everything fits in to a tapestry of energies bigger than
we think ask a butterfly what's a caterpillar ask a honey
badger what's an armadillo driftin high in dreamland
floating on my pillow I saw a mile long Dragon with an
armour plated dildo fighting for his life against Benny
and the Eskimo on the dark side of the Moon and as they
fought they'd glow and then I saw a Leprechaun sliding
down his rainbow laughing to himself landing in his
crock of gold.

A baby's God is its mum in every way and form from the moment of conception till the day that you are born they say that childhood's over when you find out you will die and Christmas time is not the same 'cause Santa is a lie sorry kids to tell you this we simply made it up don't ask why do as you're told the joys of growing up they tried to make me Catholic did I give a fuck a book a Pope a crucifix a story drenched in blood a little boy who knew the world was not all doom and gloom a little boy who would not fit the Church and school regime a little boy whose father was the toughest man in town a little boy living life adventure all around I used to talk to stars at night and I knew they listened and one night they said to me son you've got a mission.

Fen Lon the Ancient One a stormin human being a lover of philosophy of verse of thought of reason want a man to lead the charge Fen Lon steps up first fearless peerless fighting to the last a winner who knows the game and loves its mindless twists a drummer who feels the beat the rhythm knows the tempo the dancers with feet on fire can feel the futures' echo lead on show the way no man stops the party that has only just begun a bright and brave new century will any man dare call time on humanity's progression even when the Sun comes up the music keeps on pumping a cargo train at top speed is merely a fraction of the glory and the majesty channelling aggression into something wonderful musical confession a thousand people dance as one the Angels cheer from Heaven.

What happened to the ladybirds where have they all gone what happened to the heroes who will sing their song what happened to the righteous ones or are they all now wrong Heaven's Gate is in your mind it's open if you want it and all life's treasures yours to find true beauty lies beyond it have you the heart to realise a dream is but a mirror the Universe is all around you are at it's centre a mother's love is so profound the Gods are sometimes jealous the winds of change diamond edged shred through your mental cobwebs if every person on this Earth reached their full potential think of what we could achieve the party would be mental the DJs are our saviours now the beat our new communion feet of flames hearts on fire bring on the revolution.

Alcohol's a lovely drug it really dulls the senses strips away the social mask and polite but vague defences in some it brings out the truth in some brings out the bastard in me it brings out the clown and I love getting plastered start off with a couple of pints some wine then maybe champers then hit the scotch move onto rum let's get the party started four a.m. proves the man if he is still standing the Sun comes up you're walking home a night of drunk abandon an alcoholic a hardened drinker are really the same person one simply enjoys a drink and one gets stressed about it and yes one could live one's life avoiding drink completely but why on Earth enjoy yourself this is not a dress rehearsal and if you're brave come sit with me I'll drink you under the table.

And what of coke it's just a joke a crutch for little egos
and heroin now that's a sin avoiding life completely
speed is just a drug for kids and what a fucking
comedown popping pills the dance floor kings all loved
up and gurning it is a very social drug so why is it illegal
everyone I know smokes dope and all of them enjoy it
so many lovely afternoons high as a kite and smiling but
what of acid don't ask me I just could not advise you acid
opens doors in your mind whatever lies behind them is it
worth the risk to you to face your inner demons it was for
me I named them then and one by one I kill them once
you drop there's no going back until the trip is over do
you want to lose control and jump into the future do you
want to strip yourself of any trace of ego.

Saving for your gravestone is just a waste of time a man
should always treasure more the marvels of the mind
have you seen the sky on fire have you seen The Circus
have you been to Neverland have you felt an earthquake
have you felt the Dragon's breath have you ever listened
to your heart beat in your chest the sound of your blood
pumping once I was a little boy once I was a baby once I
swam in the sea completely fucking naked once I prayed
before I slept once I lost my mind but now I am just myself
I've left the past behind once I fell from the sky onto the
fields of Ireland although I wore a parachute it felt like I
had died I'm changing still I hope I will until I cash my
chips in when that day comes I know I'll smile another
stage of learning.

The Hamsters of the Apocalypse came strolling into town it was only me who saw them there was no one else around the other creatures of the night disappeared without a sound fourteen ten foot hamsters their leader wore a crown some were riding bicycles some on roller blades one looked like it had glow sticks hanging from its tail one was sharpening its teeth one had shaved its legs one had ears as big as himself one was painted red one was off his tits on crack one was sucking eggs one was sniffing poppers one was smokin skunk one was eating marbles and all were well on drunk and yes I blinked and thought this time I'd taken too much acid but when I heard the bastards howl I knew those fucking hamsters were real as me and brought with them a Biblical disaster.

What the Hell was I to do a single skinny fucker faced with giant hamsters going on a wrecker I thought that if I could find a wheel big enough to hold them they would forget their purpose and just go for a run but where would I find a wheel that size in the middle of the night and then I thought I should run but that would not be right the only option I could take was to stand and fight then I heard a noise I knew it straight away that crazy bastard Benny had come out that night to play and sitting on his back on a saddle made of rubber sat a limp wrist mincing Eskimo eating whales blubber I never thought I'd see the day I'd be happy to see Benny right then I could have jumped for joy the tables may have turned the Hamsters of the Apocalypse had reason to be worried.

Down the middle of the street the battle lines were drawn the hamsters dug in trenches and waited for the dawn Benny had his head-phones on groovin down to gabba the Eskimo had shit himself and was crying for his mamma as the morning sun came up the battle had begun but now the odds were on our side 'cause Benny phoned his mum Benny's ma was twice his size and twice as fucking hairy and even next to Benny that psycho bitch was scary the hamsters made the first move they growled and bared their fangs Benny just sat and smiled he knew his ma had plans the hamsters barrelled down the street headin straight for Benny right then his ma stepped aside behind her was Ben's granny armed with just a Zimmer frame she faced the hamster army.

Now it was a turkey shoot the hamsters dropped like flies Benny's gran stood her ground murder in her eyes and once again that bastard Ben farted in surprise the last two hamsters took to run Benny's ma gave chase she caught the first one by his tail and sat upon his face I hope it died instantly I didn't hear it scream its tail just flapped around a bit and stopped as Benny grinned the leader of the hamsters looked around and cried his plans a mess and hamster flesh falling from the sky Benny's gran had her fun she laughed and disappeared then his ma danced a jig and vanished in the air the Hamster King looked at Ben and knew the day was lost he ran like fuck to Hamster Hell to sulk and count the cost as silently that bastard Ben faded like the frost.

So back to my favourite subject fisting still haven't
tried it but I've been thinking we've looked at the styles
techniques and traditions I'd like to explain certain
conditions that should be in place before we start fisting
firstly fisting is not just a hobby and yes by the way I am
off my trolley an honours graduate of the Fist Fucking
College I need to describe certain equipment that one
will need before you start fisting there are just a few
domestic appliances some garden implements it's nearly
a science and after the first time if you get it right trust me
my son you'll be fisting for life first on the list some good
lubrication and then of course a strong pair of gloves
let's stick to the basics then we can move on to free style
techniques and fisting for fun.

If you're a beginner I'd avoid lawn-mowers strimmers are
iffy and so are toasters stick to a basic harness or frame
with buckles and chains and leather restraints left hand
or right hand it don't really matter a pillow's a help to
bite on or batter may I suggest you keep your mind open
relax and enjoy but keep yourself focused the experts
suggest some warming up stretches a couple of minutes
start with your ankles then bend your knees your waist
touch your shoulders keep your eyes forward stretch out
your neck and slowly so slowly straighten your back
hold that position till you feel your toes tingle then reach
out your arms forming a circle that ends hands outward
palms up at eye level then just relax and breathe through
your nose you feel the tingles rise up from your toes.

If you do this exercise a few times a day your body feels tip top and ready for play now that you feed straight from the source sit back and relax nature's own course did you know that under the ground a tree is as big as itself if you don't believe me then go suck an elf picture a thing in living proportions your mind is on fire your thoughts and emotions are one and the same both steadily focused your eyes open wide your pupils dilated a towering example a wee fraction of nature how many leaves have you got ya fucker I'd say more than me I'm only a yucca a simple house plant fed on chlorine tap water and stuck in a pot of man made earth fibre my roots only feel the cold kiss of plastic and so to you my life looks restricted my leaves don't know sunlight my roots small and twisted.

Does the seed of an oak know it's an acorn can a horse fly or look like a Unicorn why does a Griffin look like he does did they once exist or did we make them up what if you'd never heard of a camel or seen one in pictures a mythical animal just like The Yeti or Lord Lucan's body filtered by whispers where truth is just folly and everything real is clouded till morning breaks with the breeze our wee planet turning still but in circles a ball in a vacuum whose dimensions I doubt we will ever fathom whose beauty to our eyes by daylight is hidden and even at nightime shows only a fraction the vista's a picture the moment is captured when two billion boots smack off the dance floor the DJs have hooked up mainlining hardcore the dancers respond the Universe echoes.

Of all the religions men claim to follow most are just
horse shit a bit hard to swallow but why would a man
be eating horse shit don't ask me I think I'm an atheist
I know that it's smart to believe in yourself then cast
around do you need something else deep in your heart
the answers lie waiting a man is a myth until he decides
that what he believes in is truth or all lies ask the mirror
what's in the Ether that fills the space between here and
your dream world is it just pictures and sounds from the
past or is it a landscape where souls and beings laugh
and remember a time where but not when the Earth they
knew was ruled by men or maybe by women I don't
mean to be chauvinist I was born with a dick so male is
my view point call me old fashioned maybe I am then
blame my parents they made me a man.

Atheism is a strong position the open minded man
can see things as they are without all the sham and
ceremony and bullshit that faith often needs to make
belief worthwhile when most are a scam furthered by
people who've got some agenda to control minds or just
to make money if someone tries to sell you religion ask
them why and make them defend it if you were to believe
in something quite silly the world would just laugh and
might call you crazy but if ten thousand people believed
the same thing although it was crazy you just might give
in and think to yourself these guys could be right to dress
up in strange robes and fight the wrong fight but trust
me my son don't ever listen 'cause that is the basis of
organised religion nonsense is fact when all fact is fiction.

But then who am I to say that atheism is right a skinny
little fucker who thought he saw the light and yes I believe
in all the old Gods that doesn't mean I worship them or
trust them with my life I would say that some of them are
actually my friends all of them are still around we just
forgot their names a few of them I know for sure watch
us every day and laugh as all the actors forget they're in
a play and wonder if we realise there is no judgement
day these are threats that people use to make others think
their way Heaven is a metaphor it's how you see your life
an optimist a pessimist can you say who's right I know
which one of these I am and I know for sure that Heaven
is on Earth my son just beyond that door and Hell's here
too it's up to you it never rains it pours.

Never ask the Gods for help unless you really need it
this is strange advice I know coming from an atheist
if everything you had to do was effortless and easy
could you call yourself a man and where would you
find meaning remember once you learned to walk and
couldn't wait to run and now you sit on your ass your
challenges all gone if there ever comes a day you achieve
your life's ambitions then set your goals higher son and
trust your inner vision I think that I have told you once my
life is chasing rainbows but that is one of many things
I'll do before I go and yes I want to change the world I
want to make it better I want to do a thousand things that
people will remember I want to see the children smile and
run headlong at the future.

Have you ever questioned your own sexuality why do
people say the spice of life is variety this should be a
personal thing to Hell with society and what you think it
needs from you 'cause within your reality the only thing
that counts is you your pleasures and your freedom
society because it's weak always uses labels puts people
into boxes and worries what the neighbours might say
if they knew that someone's son or daughter was a
homosexual or even worse a queer but we know society
and its rules are crumbling the reason why is simply that
it can no longer function don't blame the anarchists this
time they're outside the margins like visitors at the zoo
throwing fruit at packs of monkeys the adults are the
walking dead and all the kids are junkies.

People are afraid of change afraid of something new
afraid of being left behind well I've got news for you in
ten years time this world of ours will spin upon its head
the lawyers all behind bars the politicians dead and
anyone who says hold on this goes against tradition well
you can go and fuck yourselves the kids are on a mission
we all know what is wrong we all know how to fix it but
have we got the balls to say society has twisted a parody
of itself where greed is just accepted it's every man for
himself and family means nothing a stranger is someone
to fear society is rotting but this time from the inside out
the anarchists are laughing they just have to stand and
watch the politicians baffled and all they do is make
more laws and spout vile worthless waffle.

And then the fuckers wonder why no one cares to vote
ineffectual plastic men just don't float my boat and yes
they all claim to care they care about their jobs and how
the papers portray them is this move good PR how can
the richest country in the world have people on the streets
they're unclean they're unseen please don't talk to me
although I may throw you change or buy your magazine
I really couldn't give a fuck you're in the shit not me if you
came to my house and there begged me for shelter I'd
slam the door in your face then go and get the shotgun
the country that I live in now calls itself civilised and yes it
is if you're rich but if you're not you're fucked and if you
think that my ideals are childish and simplistic yes you're
right but what the fuck it's better than being selfish.

A perfect world is there one there could be if we want
it but as it stands this world of ours kills children just for
profit capitalism an interesting system with no room for
prisoners or stragglers or anyone who's got a fucking
conscience it's dog eat dog in a brutal rat race where
charity is weakness and greed sets fast the pace and fuck
you if you can't keep up the tax man doesn't care all he
wants is his pound of flesh to feed the insatiable beast
that we think is civilised but in fact just eats small wonder
that so many men simply lose their marbles and leave
them twisted broken men who resemble only shadows
counting pennies paying bills credit ratings interest rates
low risk investments stocks and shares a whore to money
your ass in the air being fucked by banks who can't and
will not care.

In Ireland they speak of The Salmon of Knowledge a fish that knows everything but has never been to college well actually the fish himself doesn't know that much he just eats other fish and once a year he fucks but if a lucky fisherman was to catch and cook him all knowledge would be his as soon as he tucks in I know this sounds a bit far fetched but then it is a legend this story is not about the fish it's a story about men and our place in the world a fairy tale for children contains a maddening mystery and a thousand questions these stories that we learn when we are growing up are much deeper than first they seem each more than just a book with coloured illustrations to help keep our attention each one is a map I think and each one worth a mention.

And what about Peter Pan or the Pied Piper of Hamlyn Snow White and those fucking Dwarves or the story of Rapunzle in fairy tales lies history though I don't know which kind each one printed on your psyche mapping out your mind each one a step through learning a simple nursery rhyme can conjure up a million things previously unthought of and at that age one could accept a Prince was once a frog Twinkle Twinkle Little Star what the fuck is this Humpty Dumpty sat on a wall well man we all take risks Old McDonald had a farm rearing cows for burgers and some old woman in a shoe had more kids than she'd had dinners Hansel And Grettle put on the kettle Polly make the tea Susie took it off again but who the fuck is she the Billly Goats Gruff thought they were tough and so did the Fiddlers Three.

Old Mother Hubbard went to the cupboard to find her nipple clamps Little Jack Horner sat in the corner happily having a spank Little Miss Muffet sat on a tuffet eating her curds and whey along came a spider and sat down beside her and said bend over bitch I'm gay Three Blind Mice were playing dice to see who'd get sucked off while Cinderella was last seen with a pumkin shaped like a cock Old King Cole was giving head to Wee Willie Winkie while he lay in bed Jack made Jill take the pill he hated using condoms but liked to Rub A Dub with men in a tub while wanking over Rapunzle the Butcher the Baker The Candlestick Maker dressed in bondage gear and tied Jack and the Giant up in their beanstalk and fucked them until they were queer.

Goldilocks had her ass in the air Three Bears were taking turns till Little Red Riding Hood appeared and also got her ass up the wolf was eating out her snatch and pawing at her tits Three Little Pigs were lining up hoping for a fuck The Ginger Bread Man happily obliged he fucked all three then with a ginger bread smile faded back into an old nursery rhyme that was nothing but words built in two four time that only make sense to a very small child who knows nothing of death or any concept of time just liked those little books and loved his Ma's smile and didn't even care what was truth or silly lies was a feisty little fucker but was only knee high who stared out into the future with a glint in his eye and knew the world was perfect 'cause he was his mother's pride.

If the Fish Monger was asleep would you steal his fish
when you see a shooting star do you make a wish do you
believe in miracles do you believe in fate do you believe
that at the end you'll land at Heaven's gate do you
believe the Ancient Ones knew more than we know now
do you believe in an evil goat or in a sacred cow do you
believe a human being is the height of evolution do you
believe in anarchy in war in revolution do you believe
in yourself enough for you to say the world can go and
fuck itself I'm doing things my way do you believe that
learning cannot and will not end do you believe there is
a place where even time can bend past and future mixing
colours the present time to spend a moment that could
last forever a moment without end.

Do you believe a deaf composer could write amazing
music do you believe a blind artist can paint a perfect
picture do you believe we are alone in this gigantic
Universe do you think you only live to be a fucking
number do you believe that once the Gods walked freely
on Earth with us do you believe there is someone made
specially for you do you believe that your soul mate
is looking for you too do you believe in the power of
thought the power of forgiveness do you believe we're all
the same beneath our clothes we're naked do you believe
your every thought is carved upon your face do you
believe that in your hands you carry your own fate do
you believe the Universe was created just for you or do
you think we're animals this Earth of ours the zoo.

Never accept the status-quo to do so is defeatist never believe a man who says time is life's best teacher I know people twice my age who've lost the plot completely and who say with sincerity that youth today are stupid dream on little twisted men your time is at an end all you've left is jealousy and all you can do is condemn buy a shovel dig a hole I'll gladly fucking help you and dance on your graves you sorry lot your past is not our future yes we've learned from your mistakes we won't make them again beggars of favour clinging to power you know your grip is slipping this is the new millennium though we seem to have forgotten and we will be dancing in the streets when all your corpses are rotten new heroes will come to rewrite the script love compassion and honour.

Come another turn of the screw the day will bring the man out of the child with fire in his eyes the kids have got a plan compassion for all humanity will be the next great movement the hippies tried it in the sixties but got too stoned to march on don't worry guys we'll carry the torch I thank you for your vision the system that time was just too strong but you began the trickle that slowly but surely is building to a raging fuck wild river will any man be stupid enough to challenge a force of nature anyone who gets in the way will be stripped skinned hog-tied and fist fucked idle the hours in your ivory towers the waters are rising around you and soon all will be swept clean away the walls the foundations mere echoes the river is bringing the dreams of our children and with them a new brighter future.

Quiet now Little One you'll hear the river calling once I
was a child like you a snowflake in a snow storm what
am I now I'm not so sure the wheels are still in motion
learning and living day by day a wee fish in the ocean
I know the ocean is my home the place that I was born
to swimming 'round with fish like you and smiling when
I see you and do I know I live in water well no I wouldn't
say so it doesn't taste of anything it's odourless and
see through do I have a memory to be honest I can't
remember do I feel emotions sometimes but I try not to
have I thought about my death yes but do I care I know
I'll smile when that day comes just like I smile today life is
simple for a fish and could be so for you open your eyes
switch off your mind don't think just feel and do.

If there is a voice in the back of your mind questioning
what you do tell the fucker to shut up 'cause he wants
you to lose remember you are an animal your first and
one true nature and all the paranoia and self doubt is
conditioned human behaviour looking back from the
mountain top the path I walked is varied and often
turning back on itself and often fucking scary and all of
it I walked alone for that is the only way but now I see in
the distance across another landscape another fucking
mountain top and beyond a thousand others and so my
journey starts again if I lived ten thousand years I'd never
see everything and sometimes I find tears welling up in
my eyes the beauty in this world has the power to break
my heart just like a little girl's.

Another day another scene the painter and the picture are the same part of each other only perceptions differ inner space and outer space are part of the same spectrum one can't exist without the other this world is a reflection of how we choose to portray things and how we define its colours the Universe surrounds us all but you are at its centre I know I've said this before but this is quite important what do you think your eyes are for the most complex human feature existence looking at itself from one unit's viewpoint in this life we learn so much though we might not realise the Cosmos admiring its natural beauty through one human's eyes only a fool is not in awe only a fool is blind miracles are fucking real and surround you all the time glaring staring perfectionism the mirror is your mind.

And do you feel a part of it or do you feel alone immortal quantum particles or just skin and fucking bone even when we split an atom something else remains we cannot in fact destroy at all we simply rearrange in the flux of energy the patterns decide what form an energy will take and for what length of time the machine that sits writing this knows itself as human but how can that mean anything when all I am is atoms that have decided just for now to gather in one place a blink in time my life span though I'm glad it happened I sat one Wednesday afternoon contemplating Saturn as camels raced around its rings I wished I'd had a camera I thought I caught a glimpse of Benny playing chicken with a comet the Milky Way sat back and laughed the Universe a rabbit.

The Free Wheel Lesbian Badger Horde with left wing political opinions ambled west led by ten and followed by their minions the ten immortal badger Queens each the size of donkeys had scars from many battles won and all wore purple leggings it had been over two hundred years since the last great badger migration they were looking for new lands to hunt a new home for the badger nation they set off from the east of China turned left and gang raped the entire of India all before dawn on the first Tuesday northward then into Pakistan left a pile of rubble and entered Afghanistan there the Taliban put up a good fight but in the end it was futile to resist the badger might north once more heading for Russia Shifter took the lead howling Perestroika.

Dawn on Wednesday Moscow was a shambles south girls south let's go and get some Arabs Pinkie led the vanguard down the Caspian Sea took Iran by surprise crushed Iraq and flattened Turkey now the Horde was moving after rinsing Saudi Arabia assembled by the Red Sea shores and swam over to Africa Cardigan flew the flag as they ravaged Ethiopia half of them went south to take care of Somalia and when they got bored trashed the whole of Kenya the other half went north through Sudan Egypt and Libya the Horde reassembled on the plains of central Africa and by Thursday afternoon had got as far as Namibia in the smoking ruins that was left of Botswana the badgers stopped to rest do their hair and wax their armpits.

Friday a.m. the Horde had reached Morocco Europe
quaked in its boots the Badger Horde unstoppable
Spain and France the first to fall but no one really cared
it was a frenzied free-for-all the badgers killed and
raped although some of them stopped a while to do a
bit of shopping most of them focused on carnage death
and bloodshed the Germans didn't stand a chance the
Italians fared much worse the Swiss gave up instantly the
Belgians shit their pants the Dutch jumped into the sea
the Danes hid in the trees the Norse prayed to all their
Gods the Fins were on their knees only the Swedes stood
a chance 'cause badgers hate Ryvita they covered their
bodies in the stuff the badgers wouldn't eat them next on
their list of course the lovely isle of England.

In the quietness of suburbia the nation held its breath
they knew the Horde were coming they knew that it
meant death the airports were in chaos as people tried
to flee the Government sat on its hands and formed a
new committee to discuss the implications for the people
of the country a million people killed themselves rather
that than face the wrath of left wing lesbian badgers on
the war path the English Channel blackened as they hit
the water a boiling mass of badgers while on the cliffs
of Dover wearing boots and doing his dance that crazy
bastard Benny came out to take a stance and on his back
the Eskimo again had shit his pants the Sun was shining
in his eyes so Ben put on his Oakleys and through their
tinted lenses he saw the task was hopeless.

Sometimes I lose a hold a me brock but I'm glad to say not often my mojo is with me every day but at times I have forgotten livin life in top gear chewing up the road requires a certain kind of focus well that's what I now know your body contains everything that you will ever need and only works at its best when burning at top speed Three Little Buddhas came to me and asked me for advice what could I tell them but do as you do and know what you're doing is right they already knew this but life's often the same we all already know how to live but if something goes wrong we can blame someone other than ourselves for our sorry situation or blame the Gods and scream at the sky oh Lord oh my Lord why me your fate is your own trust me my friend there in your hand is the key.

If you had the chance to travel in time just once and just for one minute would you check out the past or look into the future or could you make that decision I know which one I would do but I'm not about to tell you I've never been to a fortune teller that might give you a clue there is a greater power than this and that power is perception all that has happened and all that will be can be seen right here in the present a million possibilities the laws of cause and effect all of the answers contained within the rules as simple as chess the board might not be black and white the pieces might look different but the game is the same and while you are playing play only to win and play brilliant 'cause somewhere inside all of us hides an all knowing and all seeing genius.

To me life is a spiritual journey and all the rest is side-
show material possessions emotional tangles can't fulfil
if inside you're hollow society demands a certain facade
and shuns expressions of feeling the ridges of modern
day life a performance a play devoid of meaning how
often have I cried for the world how often have I mourned
how often have I clawed at the earth how easy is it to lose
hope how many times have I felt and was sure there's no
light at the end of this tunnel only to find out that I was
wrong next to that light the Sun is a candle each time
I find within myself somewhere the strength to go on a
memory perhaps of that time this feisty wee fucker was
born and though my eyes have once seen my death my
love for this life keeps me strong.

And so here I sit enjoying my life in fear of my own
potential and how many times have I peeked over that
wall and known that to jump was essential do I believe
in gravity do I believe in physics do I believe in sanity do
I believe in biscuits do I believe in alcohol do I believe
in death do I believe in shadows and dust do I believe
blood is red do I believe in energy do I believe in sex
do I believe in life ever after do I believe that the dance
is older than humanity older than the sea older than
anything our tiny wee minds can conceive do I believe
that once we were fish before dry land was born do I
believe that we are alone while past through our future
lives on and would you believe a man is a ghost a ghost
is a soul going home a King will always feel like a King
regardless of castle or throne.

The Hellfire Club were doing lunch this time the middle classes got it right in the ear from the gentleman with glasses these fucking suburban hopefuls he said should all be given scooters instead of blocking up the roads with their spotless Landrovers now who do they think these people are fooling I've got a Landrover but only for shooting or perhaps when doing a spot of fishing if I'm going to town I'll just take the Roller it's a fucker to park but a man needs his comfort and you wouldn't believe the things I put up with a stampede of Landrovers going round in circles four ton of machine just to move one small woman and perhaps sometimes a few bags of shopping on the half mile round trip and on the way blocking every road it's simply disgusting.

Now how can a Landrover be a status symbol if you haven't even got the country house to go with it instead parked outside a little brick prison just like the one next door with two square foot of garden and all the eyes behind those tacky lace curtains looking out to see if those fucking bastard Jones' have gone and got themselves some new suburban must-have screaming inside dying of boredom totally enthralled by the God of television all far too concerned with keeping up their image to do something wild even if they really wanted then what's the fucking point of living in a body that's capable of anything and loves absorbing knowledge I've met people with less to say than a common garden cabbage how can people live this way what's the point to whose advantage.

The topic was a favourite of the Sergeant Major General
another old money man from the right kind of family
who fondly remembers the good old days when people
knew their station you can buy the land the house these
days you can even buy a title but you'll agree my learned
friends you cannot buy good bloodline these days
anyone with the cash can send their sons to Eton I say
it makes a mockery of a fine old institution there was a
time when school meant more than simply education your
school was more like a home and a place of preparation
for a life in the ruling class and to learn appreciation of
the better things in life and of course to forge relations
with other people of lineage whose great names built our
nation into the greatest Empire in modern civilisation.

The Hellfire Club were going strong and lunch had only
started Sir Edwin Elvin Bag Adeer was knocking back
the champers born and raised in India a lovely old
eccentric who seldom had too much to say but when he
did he meant it excellent foie gras pate he mumbled to
the waiter who just smiled as he always did they were
his favourite table they always left a decent tip and never
were complainers well not about the restaurant just about
the world in general but at least they had something to
say and didn't hide their feelings world wise hardened
thinking men who felt and with good reason society is
just a shell and life is losing meaning our time is fading
now my boys it seems these days the media are the ones
who call the shots and celebrity means genius.

Have I felt the changeling scream waking from a walking dream and all the madness in between fading now where beauty's slipstream carries you and every day seems quite surreal the world's the same but all so different and never quite what you expected the little things now in perspective mean so much more than they did yesterday it seems your eyes are working better your senses honed sharpened faster just as if you'd taken acid where learning starts the river's rapids behind you now that life meanders through the valleys of your mental landscape and if you wish you can paddle or if you prefer sit back and amble either way you're moving forward to who knows where but when you get there you'll laugh to think that once you were scared.

Of reflections of yourself in others' eyes the mirror cracked or so you thought but that could not be the mirror's made of woven moonbeam strong as light clear as could be once again it's your perception which defines all reflection and trust me all is sheer perfection all are heroes none are victims self empowerment is addictive learning through your animal instincts can one man make the difference can one man go the distance can one man live his existence to the max with child like innocence an open smile seeing always only good things hearing always echoed symphonies screaming life is as it should be a lesson learned from three monkeys contains all knowing a man will ever need true to himself in the eyes of eternity can one man create his destiny.

Evil is after all just a word just like love four little letters
human hopes human needs human words for human
deeds humans revel in their own complexity we humans
are our own worst enemy always doubting always
questioning never content with our countless blessings
always searching always seeking always unsure of our
place in the Universe our place is here on this fucking
planet do what you love and love fucking doing it and
who gives a shit if they call you a weirdo they are
blind and totally see through I know it's hard to be
an individual when everybody else grips tight to their
blindfold face your fear and do it anyway you won't
know till you try and fuck it even if you fail at least you
took a shot the bastards can't take that away.

Suck it and see now there's a good motto if at first you
don't succeed then suck a little harder sorry if that's crude
but then I am a filthy bastard with no respect at all for
people who are cattle afraid to live afraid to do battle
with their own inner demons they're only fucking shadows
afraid of the dark afraid of themselves afraid to fail afraid
to go to Hell afraid of the future afraid of the truth afraid
to understand the rebellion of youth afraid of change
afraid of the game afraid to gamble afraid to go insane
afraid to lose control afraid to take a chance afraid of the
drummer afraid of the dance afraid of attention afraid
to make a difference afraid to face the Sun afraid of the
Universe the fear of being born remains always with us
but if you're reading this you're half animal half genius.

Meanwhile back in the Garden of Eden Adam said to Eve what's this I'm eating Eve said honey it's only an apple I got it from the tree in the middle of the garden I was chatting to a snake he did seem rather friendly apples on trees are there for the taking suddenly they realised they were both fucking naked glanced down at each other and thought it was shameful Eve went back to the snake in the tree and said here ya little bastard you've fucking tricked me now me and Adam have to leave Eden those fucking apples were not meant to be eaten the snake just laughed and said tough shit honey it's my garden now you'd better get running and you'd better find something to cover yourself although may I say you've got a lovely ass a strange but simple story to describe the sex act.

Now why is such a natural thing shrouded in mystery only a mislead fool would think the Bible is actually history those stories are metaphors for human development after all how can two people have six billion descendants many things we just accept because we are told by our elders when we're young and how is a child to know that his elders can be wrong 'cause they were tricked when they were young don't believe a thing you read or hear or fucking see the only truth is inside you a truth that you can feel deep within your guardian watches every move and will let you make mistakes but never let you lose here's to you don't get screwed your future is your baby but like I say don't trust me only you can save you and then someday you'll realise how strange the things that make you.

Only you can really grasp the power of your potential
only you can search inside only you can measure only
you can understand your life your past your future only
you can hear the child screaming for its mother as they
cut the cord the world changes 'cause another actor
walks out on stage his lines learned in the Ether the plot
not fully understood till closing time and curtains the
story changes instantly the actors changing costume the
audience applaud as they are carried by the fervour
but somewhere stillness shadows all and somewhere
shadows blend and somewhere magic rings the bells and
somewhere children dance somewhere a man becomes a
man and dares to take a chance the drummer nods to the
line up and so begins the dance.

Somewhere is simplicity somewhere there is strength
somewhere there a man can see beyond his life and
death somewhere beauty lives in all somewhere eagles
dare somewhere truth is made of steel somewhere
somewhere somewhere somewhere echoes come to life
somewhere poets dream somewhere shadows turn to dust
somewhere in between somewhere pain is just a word
somewhere blood is red somewhere life is just a game
somewhere we're all dead somewhere music never ends
somewhere love begins to turn the tide and deep inside
the future and the past create a tapestry that glows and
then one feels at last the sky belongs to anyone and
everyone at once the Sun comes up the day begins but
nothing slows the dance as beauty mirrors truth in all and
one man takes his chance.

I've always known which way is north I've always known my name I've always known a players life revolves around the game I've always known freedom's worth I've always known the value of human warmth and happy thoughts and people you could talk to I've always known that life and death are parts of the same circle and yes I grieve when people pass but grief in truth is selfish within this crazy world of ours your friends are your true wealth energies multiply when people get together even if only to sit and drink and comment on the weather the art of conversation and yes it is an art a smile can mean many things a smile can break your heart a smile can bring a man to life and remind him of that time when he was a little boy that boy that's still inside.

What price these days for peace of mind what price a good night's sleep what price is one man willing to pay to see our world at peace what price to put on human life what price a mother's love to watch her child starve to death while around the world a flood of money turns in on itself and the ones who claim to own it often do I cry for the world often do I bleed and deep deep down a rage begins a rage that will not heal all the troubles of the world but by Christ I'll fucking try can one man bring compassion to a world Hell bent on greed will our species ever learn we can only grow together will men in power ever try to change things for the better love is such a simple thing love is all that counts love has brought me to my knees then love on fire rebounds.

The game goes on the world revolves the future's getting
brighter because of people like you and me we'll heal
this world together the IMF the USA OPEC and the Banks
play puppeteers with whole countries just like a game
of chance but these are people's lives at stake these are
mother's sons how can Britain justify selling children
guns are politicians being paid millions by companies
who make arms there's blood on your hands children's
blood you'll never wash it off and when you go to sleep
at night think on that you cunt think of the bullets your
companies make think what they do to flesh the skull of a
child smashed in two while you lie in your bed fuck you
ya bastard justice will come think of a mother's pain no
matter how often you wash your hands that child's blood
will remain.

Raining blood from the sky the Earth itself is bleeding
the horror of war the carnage we've brought to others
of our species can a man who is a father and loves his
own children dearly unleash the armoured dogs of war
and call the bloodshed a victory a victory for what what
Gods demand this none of the ones that I know there's
true strength in love and love conquers all and far off in
the future people look back in horror and fear at what we
have done to each other these dark dark days are ending
now and slowly we are learning to see beyond borders
and nationalism this beautiful world is a village and we
are all neighbours who must live in peace and share
and prosper together join hands with me and cry for the
world and through tears the power to heal.

Are there wild places on this Earth are there wild people who roam them are there people who are slaves and masters who claim to own them are there still Shaman Magicians and Druids who are with us but just not in costume are there Pixies Fairies and Elves if not then where did they come from are there still Gargoyles Goblins and Trolls I'd love to see a Unicorn and what about Vampires Sprits and Ghosts are they imagination we know there are heroes villains and thieves tyrants killers and madmen there'll always be fools sinners and whores hunters and farmers and badgers there'll always be mystery wonder and awe and always new inventions there'll always be music for those who can hear and for me there's always adventure.

There'll always be moonlight magic and dreams and always human endeavour there'll always be planets comets and stars and always things we will treasure there'll always be more than we've ever known forming in the Ether there'll always be energy fire and strength and always some new crazy challenge there'll always be people who say no you can't and then always ones who are willing to say go to Hell and spin the wheel on which rests their last fucking shilling there'll always be winners losers and time for both of these to consider where to go now what move to make next in dream time all this paints a picture for those who can see within the frame the answers provide the questions a man will be poor until he decides to take stock and count all his blessings.

A ship in a bottle tells its own story the one at the helm must decide to tack or to sail to pitch or to bail and when to batton the hatches only a sailor will ever see the ocean at its full glory or know how it feels to reach land at last or dream to the sound of the dolphins only the Albatross can lead the way and there only sailors can follow where daylight and moonlight blend into one the horizon as it's slowly swallowed becomes a flat line distant as time but quietly sparkles with promise chasing the sunrise west round the world the ships mast and sails cast a shadow in which dolphins swim and echo the dreams of many ships they have followed their ocean is deep its music is real we might never comprehend it how great it must feel to stand at the wheel and know mystery is real true and endless.

A flick of a coin a traveller decides which fork he should take at the cross-roads a sailor however has no such pleasure but can only go forward and windward and hope that the tide will keep him aside from rocks wrecks icebergs and pirates sometimes it's calm sometimes it's wild and always the ocean's the master the Albatross flies ahead in his skies the sailor forgets his own name so long since he heard it spoken aloud his feet know the feel of the water sailing to home his wife waiting there with gifts for his son and his daughter his heart swells with pride as he rides the tide slow straight and sure to his Island and soon in the distance a coastline appears as homeward the Albatross guides him this voyage over safe with his cargo as he thanks the Gods of the ocean.

Cereals are good for you they're full of carbohydrates cigarettes I'm not so sure so I've cut it down to twenty alcohol is medicine but only in large doses dieting is a waste of time since all diet foods are processed and any goodness they might have had long gone why not eat the labels this modern obsession we've got with being healthy completely misses the point body and mind develop together a unified self contained process balance balance that is the key your body will find its own rhythm nurture your strengths watch as they grow and never deny yourself pleasure eating is a basic need worry's the one to watch out for counting calories is like counting sheep pointless useless obsession remember the animal inside your skin the beast that will feed if you let him.

Snarling growling baring its teeth a beast with no fear and no morals that's what you are we kill and we breed and protect at times we feel threatened your strongest instinct is the one to survive the second to reproduce after these you can do what you like your body is yours to abuse your body's a temple perhaps it might be but please don't forget it's stronger than steel we now inhabit the entire fucking planet adapting and changing with need we're like a virus and nothing can stop us except maybe stupidity nuclear bombs are simply wrong I don't think we will ever use them until we have learned to harness the power created by nuclear fusion then space will be ours the planets and stars are waiting for us to explore them it's already begun and soon we will have our first international space station.

From caveman to spaceman in the blink of an eye the
Guardians watch and smile as their children invent
new toys and then there's old Father Time swinging his
pendulum back and forth and never in a hurry from
slow time to real time to space time to him a second is a
century one thousand years all in a minute a billion might
pass just at breakfast Einstein's Theory of Relativity is a
theory and nothing more Newton's Law keeps our feet on
the ground but without it would we all just float Galileo's
ideas cost him his freedom thanks to a small minded
Pope Darwin was a radical genius way ahead of his time
and Da Vinci was a freak of nature but again was only a
man names such as these tower over our history but their
work has only begun.

Sun dazed nights at the honey club therein lives
inspiration the craziest people I've ever known fly the
flag for the clubbing nation a nation without boundaries
without borders without rules without colour without
language except of course the music everyone a part to
play and every part being vital to the final piece being
played strange heavenly recital for miles around they
hear the sound the echoes causing tingles down your
spine and in your mind the player starts to gamble
a vision of what could be emerges from the shadow
dancing till the Sun comes up the DJ keeping time the
beats roll on the future's son feels at last alive the slate
is clean you're free to dream and dreaming to survive a
life of treasure yours for free a life where truth's sublime
dreaming future history the Guardians just smile.

I thought I saw a puddy cat in fact it was a wookie I dreamed that I had woken up I dreamed I was a cookie I dreamed of children made of steel I dreamed of towers of ice I dreamed there was a prize out there for which I had to fight I dreamed that many animals lived inside my skin I dreamed that life was just a game a game that I could win I dreamed that I had died before I dreamed it was in battle I dreamed I was a child again playing with a rattle I dreamed my Mum was young again before she met my Father I dreamed I had a second chance I dreamed I was a martyr I dreamed the future happening I dreamed the past dissolved I dreamed I saw a mountain top I dreamed that I jumped off then floated slowly to my death and dreamed my death was warm.

Open hands unmade plans free to drift and wonder beauty all around me now beauty without boundary open eyes mesmerised the stillness of a moment and everything contained within everything in motion a life a blink what made me think that I was just a number shadows slowly fade to dust a mask gone ripped asunder out in the mist I heard my name echoing like thunder and still I know I'm just like you a feisty little fucker and whether you decide to play or sit upon the benches is entirely up to you for both paths have their dangers but only one has true rewards and only one adventure only one can make you strong and only one brings learning I can't tell you what life's about I can't give you the answer but I know that inside you waits patiently the dancer.

Inside you a giant waits to be woken up and when he wakes the Earth will quake and will you give a fuck if some monkey says to you you can't don't even try lift your chin look straight ahead the world is now your oyster your hands can do anything that you put your mind to set your sights and set them high 'cause trust me time is wasting the future will not wait for you you have to go and take it fearsome as a man should be fearless focused energy building building gradually feeding off itself adapting changing bending breaking all the rules the fools are making run like fuck the future's waiting for the man once a shadow now a living force of nature always learning always growing bite the bullet shed your skin the player bets the player wins.

Life is hard it's meant to be if not then you're not trying any fool can cruise along and let others set the pace but when you die we will forget your name your work your face what will be your legacy how will you have helped this crazy fucked up race of ours understand itself an average life is that all and everything you want well if so off you go and be a boring cunt wear your mask just fit in and when you die good luck and don't tell me you're nobody that's bullshit and you know it you are your parent's legacy their hopes are yours to carry in your veins runs their blood you're unique so feel it a legend lives inside you an epic story tell it a fire burns inside you an ocean couldn't quell it a child was born and screamed I'm here that first scream was his loudest.

Adversity if it doesn't kill can only make you stronger
life will teach many lessons the greater ones being
harder I've seen things I don't believe I know the world
is stranger than we ever thought before I know that
there are dangers when you tear your mind apart to
see what you are made of madness is a state of mind
sanity is relative to how the human race behaves and
what's considered normal majority rules this is true what
of the individual the greatest men of our time began life
as outsiders where their minds were free to roam and
learn from different sources the playground of your mind
contains infinite new knowledge only you can seek it out
only you can share it and only when you're free of doubt
will you begin to use it it's all inside trust me now stand
up who is a genius.

Memory fading slowly now there's too much in a moment
to allow time for thought on things we've no control of a
prime example being the past what's done is done just
lose it whatever you've done brought you here to where
you now are standing circumstance good or ill what can
you do about it now's your chance to lead the dance
the future's yours don't doubt it spinning slowly in your
mind the pieces of the jigsaw all of which fall into place
if you just place the first one and remember that a jigsaw
was once a solid picture a simple puzzle that is all and
somewhere you remember what that picture should look
like its every shade and colour branded deep onto your
mind the pieces all have numbers do you recognise the
face staring out in wonder.

Looking out at the stars and thinking of that time the world was pure and innocent and I was just a boy it all belonged to me alone its beauty mine to hold those stars were bright when I was young the Moon a changing feature but all was mine and in my mind before I knew of jigsaws the smell of air the feel of grass the quietness that was night time my Mother's smiling beautiful face my baby brother sleeping dying embers in the fire our little house was creaking as I settled down to sleep the warmth filling my body knowing that if I woke up my Ma was there to mind me a three year olds' dreams are sweet the simple joy of living the safety and security of my house and village with games to play and loads of food and brothers to protect me.

I miss that crazy little boy I miss his smile and vigour I miss the sound of his laugh his sparkling eyes I wonder if a man can regain the purity of childhood is that why we all love kids because they can remind us of how amazing life can be feeding on simplicity at worst you'll maybe scratch your knee and marvel at how quick it heals a little glowing golden boy the apple of his Mother's eye the first time that I saw the sea a world of possibility opened out in front of me and I knew across the water a world was there for me to conquer perhaps one day I'd sail away the salt sea breeze upon my face all I needed was a ship some food the wind and that was it to sail away just like my Father did before he met my Mother the sea whispered of wild adventure far off lands and buried treasure.

They say life is short I say a day is long I know that
heroes walk this Earth and one is Babylon to some he
was a mercenary to some a freedom fighter who stood
his ground even though the odds were stacked against
him he only came at times of need and when his work
was over he disappeared like the breeze he must have
been immortal all through human history he appears in
different guises and only those who knew of him would
ever recognise him he had the strength of many men but
never had to show it his simple presence was enough
to tip the scales the man was tough attackers fell back
in despair just because they saw him there a lone tall
figure on the walls the man had power a God of war
unshakeable unstoppable he'd seen it all before.

Even the trees knew his name they bowed as he walked
past the animals were his friends too and helped him
if he asked he said he never killed a man he said he
never had to the sea would rise at his command the wind
carried his words and whispered death to any man who
dared to draw his sword the sky would darken at his will
and rain the very Dogs of Hell he could crack the ground
with his fist and lightning strike at where he wished the
heavy air would turn to fire if that was his desire rocks
explode mountains fold and all the while his eyes stone
cold and at his feet children played and knew for certain
they were safe the man they knew as Babylon was
their friend was a good man and while he laughed the
children sang a heroes song to a gentle man.

On his finger a ring of silver his teeth were made of
gold his hair grew halfway down his back and in his
hand a staff even the Guardians gaped in awe when
he unleashed his wrath the Mongol Hordes the Viking
Lords the Romans and the Greeks all had different
names for him their legends quite unique but they all
spoke of the same man they all mentioned his teeth they
all remembered how he stood when faced down by an
army they all remembered the fear they felt as slowly
they marched forward as if the very Doors of Hell were
opening before them as one by one they lost their nerve
and one by one they scarpered the horses were the first
to go and carried off their Captains the foot soldiers then
thought fuck this and ran in all directions.

Where is Babylon today ask me where's the wind that
filled my kite when I was young the answer is the same
Babylon is with us now his life the stuff of legend Babylon
will never die and always will defend us at our utmost
time of need he's standing on the walls looking out onto
the plains a one man fucking war his long black coat
his mighty hands his face of chiselled granite he sat
and told me of his life and asked me to record it lest our
people ever forget that hope will never die while men like
Babylon watch us remember there are giants all around
in every town in every fucking country there are heroes
who are every day making modern history the burden of
humanity the trials that living brings ego image fashion
sense these are little things.

The King of the Pigeons was on his afternoon snarfle
lazily digesting his lunch time snack of two whole cattle
later that day he was going into battle against his arch
enemy the Captain of the Seagulls the battle was for
territory and the right to ambush dump trucks in the
kingdom of the birds wars were fought by champions if
the outcome was a draw their tribes fought to the death
the Pigeon King thought he would win he was feeling
rather cocky he'd never lost a fight before his friends all
called him Ricky although he was merely one inch tall his
size beguiled his might a black belt in nine martial arts
the fucker loved to fight he was as bald as an egg and
had tattoos across his wings one that said Death From
Above and one that said Fuck Chickens.

The last time that their champions met the outcome was
a draw a bad result for both sides that kicked off the
Twelve Year War in which eighty million birds were killed
and many more were wounded the bird that now was
Pigeon King was born during that conflict he'd seen his
friends and family killed and seen the pigeons bested
now it was his chance to fight and regain pigeon honour
for without honour a pigeon is no better than a swallow
to be laughed at as they walk the streets heading for
McDonald's the only skips they were allowed since
they signed the Feathered Treaty at the time they had
no choice it was that or face extinction at the hands of
seagull bands pressing home their victory now Ricky had
within his grasp the chance to re-write history.

I doubt there's ever been before a pigeon quite like Ricky
he never used to shit on cars but pick them up and throw
them sometimes at moving trains if he wanted to de-rail
them this he did just for fun he was no fan of humans but
in the main his hatred was aimed at those shag bag shit
head seagulls his favourite trick was to wrap their legs
round their necks then wing fuck their miserable skulls
years ago he had lost count of the number he had killed
but even a million would not be enough to make up for
the pain he had suffered even when he was only an egg
he felt the shame of his species and vowed there and then
to champion them and rebuild the great Pigeon Empire
he flexed his wings sharpened his claws polished his
teeth and scratched his balls.

Meanwhile out at the far side of town the Seagull Captain
and his mates sat around psyching themselves up for
the ruck the stakes might be high but Percy was tough or
Percy the Pigeon Slayer as he preferred to be called a
hardened veteran of the Twelve Year War he also hated
the Feathered Treaty but for an entirely different reason
when the gulls were winning the war he and his band
wanted to kill them all pigeons are scum they deserve
to die or at least have their wings broken rats of the
air that's all they are a sky without pigeons would be
better by far he then said his prayers and took to the air
knowing he'd find that bastard Ricky somewhere flying
the lead in a complex formation the sky was blacked out
by the whole seagull nation.

The Badger Horde was near the shore Benny didn't flinch
he'd been in much worse spots before and didn't give
an inch as the badgers reached the coast he danced a
wee bit harder which sent rocks flying off the cliff and
each one hit a badger he danced himself into a flurry
his mighty body a whirlwind but no matter how many
Benny killed the bastards just kept coming as they began
to scale the cliffs Benny increased his assault he charged
along miles of coast the death toll doubled per minute
the sea was red with badger dead as night began to
close the badgers decided to fall back and attack again
at dawn back to Europe's coast they swam a dejected
badger swarm their planned invasion now hit a wall
thanks to an unforeseen problem.

In the morning Benny was gone he was tired of killing
badgers they gained a hold on England's coast and
moved inland with vengeance they raped and pillaged
plundered and killed and stole the fucking Landrovers
London was reduced to rubble and in fact it looked much
better in retrospect the Badger Horde had done the world
a favour in Scotland men hid under their kilts in Wales
they hid behind leeks a clever deception but not quite a
weapon and all were found within weeks the entire island
had been destroyed not even a cow remained the whole
countryside a desolate wasteland covered with heaps of
bones ah yes indeed my dear and brave England you
won World War One and War Two on Hyde Park Corner
the Artillery Men stand stock still unshaken unmoved.

To Ireland and America the badgers turned their sights
a little island a bit of a swim should not be much trouble
Trevor launched the aquatic attack and landed just
outside of Dublin he and his comrades attacked the
bars and there discovered Guinness that was the end of
the war for them 'twas quite a sight to witness badgers
getting pounding drunk all along the Liffey come the
night it was party time the city started kicking half a
million badgers drunk and now as placid as kittens
back in England the Badger Council heard about what
happened and decided to go and check it out and reign
in their stray battalion when they hit town they were met
by the sound of badgers singing Dixie and thought what
the Hell we've wrecked half the world let's cut loose kick
back and party.

The following morning a hungover army lay on the streets
of Dublin the Badger Council had decreed 'twould be a
shame to wreck such a country the Badger Horde still in
their millions moved west across the island on the way the
pubs of Ireland gladly provided refreshments the doors
were swung open the Guinness kept flowing the badgers
were treated like tourists as on the west coast the great
badger host assembled and practised their backstroke the
swim would be long but badgers are strong as one they
hit the Atlantic the people of Ireland breathed a sigh of
relief they alone had been spared but on the condition
they kept brewing Guinness and sent it by raft to the
Horde the people of Ireland still scared but delighted
returned to life as before.

A thousand goats a thousand stoats a thousand sheep
and horses charged through my mind and then behind a
herd of headless arses people who I'd never met doing
things I never dreamed of in places that could not exist
right outside my window walking naked down the street
the people didn't see me living in a state of grace tall
now though once a Pygmy and in the crowd a smiling
face told me how life should be a carnival where animals
could speak and if they wanted could change their shape
a naked ape called me on my mobile and said man get
a grip this life's a trip the rest's a fucking side-show that
smiling face came back to me and then I recognised it
and every wrinkle on his face told me my life story the
face was me but who else could lead me to life's glory.

A friend in need a friend in deed a friend should be
forever a friend to love a friend to hug a friend who
knows you better than you do yourself sometimes that
friend was once a stranger who you let into your life
regardless of the danger that you face when you say tired
friend lean on my shoulder are you strong are you selfless
and willing to believe that someone else will lend you
help regardless of your need that someone else will watch
for you while you are asleep and will always help you
grow will always hold the line will rest with you on the
path when your feet are tired will stand by you in a fight
will never let you down and when you die will dig your
grave with his own bare hands your last glimpse that
smiling face that stranger in the crowd.

Happiness is all we ask but can you pay the price travelling far within myself my toes an infinite distance from my ears and in between a world of truth existing that elusive bastard happiness the world's most sought out thing don't look at things surrounding you look instead within life's a bitch this we know it's time to play the game push yourself you will grow a wee bit at a time nature has one simple goal don't bother asking why such questions are for fools my son you're here and now sunshine everyone I meet or see if only for a minute teaches me something new though I might not understand it that is how I play the game for you it may be different but so what we're just the same we're giants raised by Pygmies to learn to grow to reap to sow your life can make the difference.

Skin's a strange and wonderful thing you'd look quite strange without it but what does it say about yourself a lot perhaps don't doubt it your skin is the person your skeleton wears your first mode of expression it can be controlled or live laisse faire entirely at your discretion your skin will tell all there is to know the first layer of confession your skin shows your age if that's what you want your toes your knees your nipples will speak to you tell you what to do unless you are a cripple I am an evolutionist I am a born again baby I am a revolutionary a child of atomic anarchy I firmly believe a man is a myth unless he's got a dream I firmly believe that love conquers all I firmly believe I believe a man is just shadow a ghost until what he believes feels real.

He's a modern day monkey a big hearted flunky a bit of all right but a bit of a junkie but what's wrong with that we all need a hobby and it helps now and then to get off your trolley get down in the muck lie in the gutter hit the bottom rung swim in the sewer get your hands dirty eating manure get a real taste of the poorest of the poor you may be quite surprised at what you can learn 'cause down in the dirt you will find a gem of pure unfiltered wisdom that makes you think again that makes you reassess your values and your goals that makes you realise that right before your nose the greatest show of all is playing to packed rows the audience are actors the actors lost the plot the director cut a few more lines and rolled a note so what.

As two by two the animals fucked upon the stage the audience then threw them scones and cheered them on hooray hooray ya fuckers give it socks fuck your little brains out go on boys have it large go on girls use strap-on's a cosmic fucking orgy is happening around us a non-stop feeding frenzy of creatures on the rut born to die born to live born to eat and fuck born into a mad mad world it gets madder by the minute the audience all naked now screaming 'cause they love it the animals saw their chance jumped off the stage and joined in it's every fucker for himself for herself whatever a pumping growling naked mass a flesh filled humping river wet with sweat a free-for-all their bodies stuck together while in the wings the director grins business sir or pleasure.

The show sold out no seats left outside the queue gets
restless they hear the noise from within their panicking
their breathless they start to beat down the doors the staff
could no way stop them they charge into the theatre and
what they see quite shocks them but not for long they join
the throng the director thinks it's Christmas the orchestra
and instruments are somewhere in the flesh pit the ice
cream vendor has been raped by a penguin with a
trumpet outside the Police have arrived they heard about
the banquet within an hour they'd been de-flowered lost
deep in the cess-pit each with their batons shoved up
their asses the law's an ass so fuck it the director laughed
to see such fun a cow jumped over a bucket into the mass
with its tail in the air and was instantly fucked by two
rabbits.

All round the City the word spread like wildfire this show
was a sure hit a must see from far out of town people
arrived in a desperate scramble for tickets but to no
avail there were none for sale the show was reaching
its climax the actors the band the animals the cops were
lost in a hypnotic trance of feeling and fucking moaning
and grunting the audience passed out as they came all
over each other and all over the furniture the curtains
were stuck to the railings the show must go on said
some whinging Pom as he was spit roast by two hairy
Australians the newspapers raved the critics heaped
praise the best show ever seen in the West End the
director said maybe as he lay in flagrante with a corpse
two whores and a turkey as curtain call came the mob
screamed refrain encore encore lets again.

A Guy called Harper was kicked to death outside a night club in Ireland he was going home on his own and saw a kid getting battered by a group of thugs scum of the earth thick fucks acting the hard man five on one nice odds boys you really proved your manhood the kid got away they turned on my guy and kicked him until he was dead life is cheap sometimes it seems ok to murder your brother if he pissed you off or got in your face or said your girlfriend was ugly my guy was simply walking home a night like many others saw someone in need and tried to help he was not playing the hero and paid with his life for doing what's right to protect someone who was weaker for this guy was strong but not strong enough now the guys who killed him are freemen.

I know this is a sorry wee story what's worse it's true and quite recent violence to some is a strange kind of fun what good is a life filled with hatred my guy's at peace now his battles all won the world will remember his name he used to write poems and loved going clubbing this world is poorer without him and those who killed him your lives are forfeit and forever your names will mean shame but what drove you to do what you did then what poison were you fed as a child what anger caused this I don't understand nor in fact do I want to we're on different planets those scum bags and me and that's the way I like it and God help us all if we ever meet I might do something I'd regret 'cause that would make me just like you and I know that's not how he'd want it.

As round the wheel turns a good man gets burned and
all we can do is ask questions or blame the Gods for our
sorry lot but Gods are slow to give answers they prefer
to sit back and watch us fall flat then see what we learn
from our lessons they could just step in and fix everything
but then forever our race would be children that's not
why we're here we've got all we need to make life on this
Earth seem like Heaven don't be afraid to break from the
cage the real world is just round the corner never give in
to do so is sin have faith in yourself and your vision far
back in the past a memory at last that place that once
was your prison with each step you take the child re-
awakes and reminds you that life is for living the truth is
out there it's mixed with the air the sunrise your smile in
the mirror.

The ones who've passed on your questions all gone I
hope you achieved all you wanted as real time refines
the past in your mind the future an unblemished canvas
the picture unfolds you look but unsure if it's you or the
paint doing the painting the shapes are familiar as are
the colours the brushes know where to go it's almost as
if the painting is finished and you're watching a film
of you doing it this world is deceptive when things are
reflected as opposites look at each other there must be
a point somewhere in between at which both of these
things merge together and looking both ways your mind
in a daze your reflection jumps out of the mirror and in
a sharp blinding flash the clocks are turned back colour
where once there was blackness.

November 1963 the death of the American Dream one man was shot the world reeled in shock except for the bastards who killed him a good man has died so many cried and with him the hopes of that era the man wanted peace this was his crime is that the fate of the noble a man of vision cut down by the blind his life gives us all example the Summer of Love is that what they called it by November the summer was over with blood on the streets tears on men's cheeks and a good man now pushing up clover strange how it goes strange that men chose to kill the man they called leader to add to the horror they then killed his brother and lastly his son to make sure that the ideals that JFK fought for would be sunk with his corpse lost forever.

Who shot JR who shot John F. perhaps it was the same person where truth becomes fiction and fact contradiction the who's and the why's all lose meaning who shot John Lennon who shot Kurt Cobain who nailed Jesus Christ to the cross these men weren't just people they were living ideals all way ahead of their time who killed them's irrelevant part of the small print in a world filled with fear they led bravely if they had kept quiet would they still be alive but men such as those never could take Martin Luther he re-shaped the future his words strong and sure as his deeds another great man though killed by a gun in fact died because they believed in a much better place for our mad fucked up race you can kill men but not their ideas courage honour dignity they played they gambled they won.

Could we stop the wind could we hide the clouds could
we make the rain fall somewhere else could we drain the
ocean could we black out the sunshine could we capture
just one little rainbow could we halt the tide could we
end the night or quench the fire of a volcano somehow I
think not we are but a dot in an infinite magical Universe
the things that we cling to are worthless and see through
in ten thousand years who will care who was richer or
poorer winner or loser or who bottled out of a dare this
planet is ancient its scars are the remnants of its fierce
fiery birth long ago when time was irrelevant calendars
unheard of in the vacuum of space all is silent our
planet's still cooling and who are we fooling when we
fight over who owns chunks of it.

The future's unwritten our species beginning to
understand our true potential this world is a cradle
and we are just babies a nuclear bomb's just a rattle
compared to the Sun and that's only one of more stars
than we can imagine in the far distant future when our
strange wild weird cultures will have moulded themselves
into one people will look back and ask themselves what
were we trying to do complete annihilation famine
starvation war after war after war untold suffering
savages butchers were once our leaders and heroes and
if war is pure Hell then who is the Devil the foot soldiers
or the Generals we'll miss JFK on that terrible day the
dreams of a decade died with him and how many died
for that nation's pride the events of that day today echo.

115

A man should have a trade a craft a passion and a
hobby an idle mind is a dangerous thing in fact it's
self destructive your creative side and yes we all have
one needs exercise like your muscles or it becomes stiff
stagnant useless but when used is a wonderful thing
with each day you grow as living unfolds an incredible
powerful vista you'll surprise yourself the cards that you're
dealt are always enough to place bets on you'll win a
little then gamble a bit more and soon you'll have a wee
stockpile of things that you value and are unique to you
are personal fulfilling and worthwhile if life makes you
horny then get up each morning and don't think about
what you did yesterday the world is your lobster your
oyster your jigsaw and it's all down to you how it works
out.

Men like Picasso Dali and Mozart were as crazy as tits
on a bull but that didn't matter those men knew better
than to listen to fools who said hold on you can't do this
it's new it's a first what gives you the right to go change
things we're happy down here simple as beer your
work makes us question our values don't rock the boat
we'll sink while you float or walk uphill while you fly
over mountains life is a challenge who dares throw the
gauntlet but who dares always wins or dies trying live fast
and die young was once the done thing but now days
things are quite different live fast and live on as each new
day dawns expand and extend your own boundaries
the strong will prevail the weak meek and frail are left
sucking their thumbs on the sidelines.

A player a spectator a pothole a crater a giant of a
man or a Pygmy are one and the same how they play
the game will dictate how history recalls them a hero
a victim a ghost or a vision a coward a great man a
martyr a success a fuck up a breeder a feeder a bastard
an Angel a wanker a genius a faker a giver a taker a
leader of men or a flocker a gambler a hedger a mouse
or a badger who cares they're just words fucking labels
headstones erode worms will eat bones your children
can sully your good name your life is a trickle a wee tiny
ripple in the ocean of life fish are equal the prey and the
killer the baker the miller the sculptor the clay the mad
fucker and which one are you the prisoner the screw the
gate the gate keeper the keys life might break you but
never give in and never fall down on your knees.

Freedom yes freedom to live as you want is as rare these
days as a virgin if you live in boxes surrounded by pitfalls
and worry what people might think then why fucking
bother the world is your oyster and inside a pearl that
is you stare straight at the mirror don't flinch blink or
quiver reflected are myriad faces they all are familiar
and strangely quite similar each one is a path you might
take the choices are yours and how many doors face
you in that long hallway where none give a clue to what
lies behind your death your salvation your birth-right
for life to mean something it will always hurt some but
it's no worse than having a tooth out go take the pain it
won't be in vain and when it's done you'll look back and
giggle ask yourself this all men take risks are we men
now or still little children.

Douglas Adams had a wonderful theory about an infinite
number of monkeys he said that if you gave them each a
typewriter they would type out the works of Shakespeare
not straight away you understand it would probably
take some time and on the way they might also type out
everything else ever written a wonderful theory you will
agree we all loved that man and we miss him strange
then to think that this little book was written by just one
with one typewriter at school my teacher made fun of me
in front the rest of my class perhaps at the time he thought
it was cool strange the strange things that shape you
harken oh ye vain glorious day fain tehood fair Romeo's
a faggot thank you good Shakespeare I now make a pigs
ear of a once great but now common language.

Evolution's unstoppable of this we are proof are we
brave enough to move on I live in the real world I watch
it evolve I've seen the cracks in the surface society
countries attitudes monkeys language warfare sex-toys
not long since the wheel was new a big deal we now
have machines to work for us and whatever next whose
taking bets we'll conquer the entire fucking Universe
the population explosion is in fact a good thing 'cause
soon our wee Earth will be knackered then we will move
on first stop the Moon then beyond that who knows it's
uncharted machines are our servants they will never
rule us if you think that you're silly and paranoid look
what we've done in the last hundred years each day
our species moves forward baby steps whatever next the
future an unblemished canvas.

Why does an ostrich bury his head in the sand or a
man stick his head us his arse bald crazy monkeys don't
know they are God-Kings we're freaks we're unique
we're fantastic but still we are learning and pushing
the boundaries of what we believe to be possible just
look around each day we are changing the future the
future she beckons come little children the pathway to
your dreams is right at your feet just step on it there's no
turning back the past is the past history can teach but not
lead in this new millennium we can wipe the slate clean
the next thousand years be our finest war is nonsense
belongs in the past-tense with religion and nations and
fear a man is a man a woman a woman their colour
their language irrelevant hatred is thought not something
we're born with don't teach it and soon it dies out.

An undiscovered country waits for the monkey the
optimists win hip hooray I laughed at those fools in those
last few years preaching the coming of Dooms Day in ten
million years we will still be here disease war and famine
lost language like Shakespeare's phraseology my Father
once told me life is a goldmine keep digging each new
thing you learn a priceless wee gem you're rich but you
don't even know it and deep in your mind the drummer
keeps time the dancer now lost in a frenzy his eyes have
rolled back his body a wreck his boots keep pounding
the dance floor dazed in a trance a part of the dance
and nothing can quite match that feeling surrounded by
strangers but no thought of danger the DJ rips free falling
hardcore the lights have come on the dancers keep going
then quietly nicely exploding.

The quadruple headed minkey of leg-ends Daywards
Teath gurning while returning from Christmas on the
beach the Sun came up he caused a ruck while skipping
down the train freedom flowers in his ass a nutshell
for a brain squirrels flying across the sky darkened the
horizon street bums calling give them guns the answers
out of reach floods of chickens selling feathers stalls with
cows selling leather a juke box singing for the weather
my shoes were lost but still together in a world of mist
and sunken treasure they came for lunch and stayed for
dinner drank the wine then broke the windows a Chinese
Box waited for them inside out the fear of boredom
drove them to fierce destruction their roots the garden far
behind them at Christmas Santa gave them heroin.

Skin up shoot up rack up line up the Elves took turns
fucking Rudolph his red nose flashing as he came off
Elvis said I want that burger lots of mayo no cucumber
two large fries and a seaweed milk-shake James Dean
said hold on it's my turn as he grabbed a hold of Marlyn
Eva Brun and Che Guevara givin head to Joseph Stalin
as he read a book on Communism smokin skunk and
drinking champagne desert rats sang in the black rain all
our heroes fucked on Valium Viagra Prozack and sugar
free chewing gum Willy Wonka had a stiffy an Umpa-
Lumpa said hold a jiffy greased his ass and bit his pillow
think of England in the summer traffic jams airport chaos
choking smog burning animals foot and mouth outdoor
festivals criminal justice armed police men.

Drinking thinking of the bastards who made the laws in the first place the King is dead who will take his place full moon night the people cheered all their heroes have turned queer wearing pink smokin gear high as kites in a hurricane the walls a mess as Hitler's brain left his skull a single bullet left JFK with seven flesh wounds do you think that we believe that yes we're fools but not quite brain dead the ice caps gone the oceans rising the whales all dead the dolphins in tins the pandas skinned the tigers foot rugs anyone fancy roast stuffed dodo gorilla stew buffalo pizza stir-fried polar bear penguin soup walrus pancakes topped with sugar elephant sandwiches whole scale slaughter we love to live but we're better at murder a rabbit smiles at the headlights.

Mao Tse Tung was a vegetarian so was I till I started eating meat again handle bars trolley cars hard boiled eggs for breakfast naked people screaming Jesus in the supermarkets politicians sharing needles outside in the car park Mother Theresa was a Ninja and a trained assassin Robin Hood's favourite fun was colonic irrigation Russian spies Jews Gentiles introverted cabbage Hindus Muslims Christians Hoodlums all as mad as carrots am I the only sane one left if so God help the Planet I stood there once on Linium and watched a supernova although I was a wee bit stoned it could have been an escort a camel humps an Arab grunts there is no doubt about it if you wanna grow then love yourself the bastards stole me trousers.

Joey the Greek was racking up lines a fiver a throw no discounts coming down hard mad paranoid there's only one way I can fix it here take a fiver cut me a nice one we're mates but business is business head down and sniff an instant clean hit there's drugs and then there's cocaine into my blood stream fast lap through my veins and straight home to what's left of my brain Joey just smiles we've been here before perhaps a million times or so it feels now that great sacred cow my ego jumped over the Moon and kicked his heels twice before landing nice on a pizza anchovies no mushrooms that Joey just bought sat there in a box with two slices missing a third one half bitten attacked by a squirrel he sounded sincere in fact I almost believed him.

What kind of squirrel I asked out of interest a red or a grey or a pinstripe male or female ears arms legs a tail raincoat crash helmet dog collar edge of town dress sense motorbike licence hair long or short had he ear rings stuck in his ears or anywhere else nose eyebrows tail backside toes and how many of those did the wee fucker have two four six eight ten or twelve did he jump down right at you out of a tree or did he hide by the bins in the alley I seen two there once ready to pounce but I was just off to the laundry I'm sure that they knew I had no food or else the wee fuckers had haved me I'm told if you whistle a bit like a chicken with its legs upside down chewing a bullet the squirrels will think that you are a mink turn and make a run for it.

Joey said maybe those bastards are crazy they've got
guns and they know how to use 'em they killed my Ma's
tortoise shelled him on purpose and left him to die in
the garden my Ma called the vet he said it's useless the
fucker's as dead as a burger but lucky he wasn't a burger
I mean 'cause if that was the case they'd have scoffed
him well that's what I told her the truth was I rolled him
around far too fast and he popped out how could I tell
her that I killed the fucker she'd have smacked me or
halved my allowance when we told my Da he just fucking
laughed the tortoise had once shit in his shoe when he
put them on his clean socks were ruined and was nearly
late for the office clean him and boil him he said while
still smiling we'll use the wee shite as an ashtray.

And that's what we did my Ma was impressed his shell
looked quiet nice on the table we still call him Harry
'cause that's what his name was to us he will always be
special but back to the squirrels those bastards are killers
they tore half the box when they jumped me I managed
to grab one his mate pulled a gun and said mister let
go of the squirrel I dropped him and ran but by that
time the bastards had got their wee claws at the pizza
they hate garlic bread or so I've heard perhaps they're
Vampires incarnate they're vicious enough if they bite
you they draw blood it happened to my cousin Sammy a
few years ago while on his way home on his own after
skating with Danny his wee brother said he was white as
a sheet and couldn't sit down for a week.

Cancer is a disease of the mind manifested on the body and once again the sceptics will say this guy's off his fucking trolley a screw loose perhaps a mental relapse crazy as ashtrays on bicycles but why would a body built for survival manifest a disease that will kill it 'cause cancer develops it is not contagious you could eat one with no ill effects the mind and the body are like Laurel and Hardy separate but one entity one lives for the other your father your mother in you are partners for life what causes cancer where is the answer the search for a cure is big business but the search for a treatment is better for business 'cause treatment costs more than a vaccine if we find a vaccine and everyone has it it's millions of pounds out the window.

Call me a cynic your right I'll admit it this world is a weird fucked up place how many countries are held down on their knees by needless cruel foreign debt they still borrow more and spend it on war or the lavish lifestyles of dictators politicks religion guns superstition genocide cruelty oppression out there every day just open the papers all we see is an edited version the truth is much worse of this I am sure but our delicate stomachs can't take it we live in a bubble the world is in trouble and not enough people care but that's slowly changing with each generation the animal fades from our make-up and with it the killer that once we all were remember it's not long since the caves how many people died young and needless and lie in cold unmarked graves.

The Unknown Soldier came over for supper his body
shredded by bullets I said you're a ghost he said fuck you
I know I've come here to ask you a question did I die for
nothing my body lies rotting my children will never be
born my family mourned for me thank God they did not
see their handsome son's ruined body they prayed I died
quick is that fucking sick when all that a mother can ask
is a quick clean cut murder for her son and his brother
and she died without ever knowing it's still going on
what the fuck's wrong was World War Two not enough
how much blood will be spilled till we learn to end it
just fucking stop are all the world's leaders cowards and
feeders we need a new era of trust please stop the killing
at night I hear screaming this tired old ghost needs a rest.

The glory of war the glory of what the glory of war you
monkey rivers of blood rivers of what river of blood can't
you see the ghosts everywhere we know war is Hell then
who is the Devil the one with the gun or the General
and who are the victims the dead or the killers can any
therapy erase the horror that comes from using a gun
against your will follow orders to maim and to kill butcher
at will in war there can be no winners just losers and
losers with one little difference some losers are dead and
some living and who suffers most the killer the ghost or
their mothers back home where they came from rivers of
tears filled over the years that burst their banks all far too
often gallons of blood mix with the mud dead foot prints
where the ground softens.

I dreamed that sunlight made me strong as the Wizzard
passed the bong first to me and then Fen Lon and then
a life size Poke-Mon whose name I cannot remember in
the last days of September the hills alive with dove tailed
rabbits chicken soup deep fried carrots naked monkeys
naked parrots bottled water low fat spread egg white
omelettes fennel tea flying carpets chocolate biscuits
used milk cartons yoghurt pots white sliced bread peanut
butter spray on starch fresh egg pasta curried lentils
small red onions Bisto gravy Lea and Perrins golden
syrup English mustard baking soda fresh crushed garlic
chilli peppers foie gras sandwiches currant buns Cornish
pasties Gruyere croutons shell fish burgers asparagus tips
crystal glasses plastic forks eat molasses.

Tired now but who cares the world's a truth the world's a
dare fill the bong with fresh skunk the Wizzard said let's
get drunk as he mixed a few martinis two parts gin one
part petrol served on ice with good olives as I looked out
over Sydney surrounded by the latest wannabes my mate
said Mike you've lost your marbles over there under that
table I said Sham forget about them I will get new ones
if I need them as Ninja crash dived through the window
he always had to make an entrance I said man just use
the staircase or perhaps the elevator waste of time was
his reply I'm half sober but I'll fix it would you risk it for a
biscuit as night time sparked with neon promise fireworks
lit up half the city the tree the tree no look what's in it.

Pain's a question in itself the Wizzard said as he dealt four new hands of five card poker twos are wild so are jokers play for money or for rounds New York hotel fourteenth floor Benny smashed through the door deal me in he demanded not a chance I retorted unless your money's on the table and did you have to bring that fucking Eskimo he's an all right kid but a wee bit cheeky drinks too much and smashes TVs just for fun when he's bored Sergeant Sniff was throwing doughnuts at the roof across from my house the neighbours musta called the filth Sitting Bull said let them in bring me wenches bring me horses bring me cyber punks on acid bring me turkeys killed for Christmas bring me demons chopped to pieces bring me home in one piece please.

As time goes by life gets stranger once a man born in a manger lost the plot and then he realised people needed to believe in something anything life is hard dare we hope for a better world yes we do and we'll make it for ourselves if we have to fake it catch a dream in your hand mother it love it make it real for yourself because you can brockin till the Sun came up the Three Little Buddas didn't give a fuck Fen Lon Sham The Ninja and Pockets Hassey me and Davy fucking Crocket Benny the Eskimo Tits just went bananas hardcore beats rocking through the Planet from London to Sydney Hong Kong Shanghai Dallas Beijing Berlin Cape Town shall we dance naked in the mountains can a man whose lost give you directions to your home if you don't know where you came from.

Chicken soup hula hoops cat flaps and gay chickens lying face down in the gutter I thought of things like Christmas I thought about my family and where they might be now I thought about eternal life another sacred cow I thought about shootin smack but a promise held me back I thought about my Mother's face and that thought gave me strength to raise my head and face the world fuck ya come on do your worst I am a man I am alive I am myself of that I'm proud I will fight any fucker and I'll win 'cause now I'm faster stronger sharper clearer focused on my goal whatever that is the grass is greener on the other side the skunk is sweeter skin up get high the future's bright and getting brighter go and get it Devil take the hind-most the ship must reach its port 'cause there are no fucking lifeboats.

No room for manoeuvre the path is straight and narrow pickin up speed swift sure like an arrow a diamond in your mind filters out the shadows clarity returns and with it Heaven's promise they're brockin on the hills and ravin in the valleys dancin in the streets tearing down the cities rippin up suburbia tradition is for pussies the adults spineless shells stand back step down fuck off you all loved David Bowie but none of you believed him 'cause if you fucking had you would just give us our freedom it doesn't matter now the pressure keeps on building and all your institutions built on false foundations the walls came crumbling down we danced upon the wreckage of a thousand years of folly the DJs melting records give it up give it up can you feel the future's echo.

I watched the Four Commandos tooled up fired up stormin I watched them beat a path through Hell and fist fuck those Four Horsemen I watched them break every rule and come out on top still smiling I watched them chewing broken glass I watched them drinking poison none of these done any harm these boys are legends giants I watched them eat a hill of beans I watched them dance in free-fall I watched the DJ's fingers bleed as he tried to keep up I watched as shadows turned to dust and children become grown-ups my mind was opened with a hammer it hurt like Hell but so what it's better than living in a cage I'm open to vibrations listening learning every second aware of subtle changes in the tempo of a world where energy's contagious.

Listen up Danny Boy the pipes are fucking calling the future's knocking on your door there is no time for packing grab your jeans and your boots forget your shirt go bare chest there are no maps for where you're going the wild out-lands await you use your wits you might survive and with a little luck you'll break through the walls you'll see they're plastic see through and beyond them who can say come back and tell us sometime or perhaps send a card to let us know you're ok out there dreams and reality are symbiotic patterns it's up to you what shape they take free will all that matters create re-make enforce your will on circumstance around you love is the law love not war and all else jigsaw pieces assemble them as you wish let loose your inner genius.

Egg sell ent Fan tas tick Won der full A may zing such
cool words when you break them down I have this thing
about words and their sounds I suppose you'd agree
since you've read this far already there is power in words
I'll give you an example God is a word that to an atheist
means little but to someone who believes it is the centre
of their being war is just a little word but conjures up
such horror if those two words did not exist what kind of
world would this be John Lennon asked that very question
he asked us to Imagine but Lennon was an idealist in a
world of brutal realists one of whom took a gun and by
shooting John proved it another human life ended by a
bullet another martyr to the cause another nail for Jesus
another six foot hole to dig into the ground that feeds us.

I often wonder why men like these die before their time
live fast die young might sound good but to die like
that's a crime I'd like to live for two hundred years but
a thousand would be better think of all the things you'd
learn and all the things you'd see all the people that
you'd meet and all the different countries that you could
live in if you wanted and learn from all their cultures and
if you said no you'd get bored then get a life you monkey
how could you be bored in this great world go climb a
fucking tree if you think that boredom's real then your a
boring person there's only one thing for you my son a
good deep full on fisting after that tell me you're bored I'll
ask then why are you grinning and by the way don't trust
doctors they just like to cut up people.

I scream you scream everybody loves ice cream behavioural patterns contained in genes perhaps my son but what the fuck does that mean your parents then their parents how far back can you go ten thousand generations perhaps ten thousand more back to pre-historic man when we lived in caves go back a little further then to when we lived in trees how many generations did we spend as monkeys and where the fuck did they come from they didn't just appear the first life forms came from the sea ok so now we're fish all this information contained within your body the answers are all waiting there learn how to ask the questions when you're awake then everything becomes real time meditation the gateless gate an endless loop describes your situation.

The mirror would not lie to me the world was upside down ugliness comes from within so smile my son don't frown you are a walking miracle whether you believe it push yourself every day expand your self made limits it's been years now since that sacred cow my ego bit the dust and left me naked in the world my senses are enough to describe to me what I am and of the senses touch is the most powerful without it I'd be fucked and probably not even know now wouldn't that be nuts but stranger things have happened me I'll tell you all about them in this little book of mine or if not in this the next one so many magic tales to tell I hope I find the time but it's tricky to describe such things within the bounds of language my story is a simple one he came he saw he partied.

Kevin the Kiwi from Hell a notorious citrus bastard was a bit of cunt when he was drunk and worse when he was plastered life is a bitch he said once when pissed I'm only playing the game as he nicked my drink then tried to convince me that the barman had picked it up his little ruse failed I knew him too well in fact since he first came to England on a cargo boat laden with fruit destined for some supermarket when he learned of his fate to be served on a plate he decided to make a run for it you see back in the crate himself and his mates believed they were going on holiday a long way it seemed from New Zealand to England but kiwis are strong and seaworthy and so three weeks later as they reached the harbour they thought here comes the trip of a lifetime.

Kevin the Kiwi thought he was fucked alone lost and broke stuck in England until I met him the wee fuck was hitching on the M1 halfway to Bristol I said jump in son wherever you're going I'll take you as far as I can he said thank you mister my feet are all blistered I've ran all the way here from Dover they were going to eat me just then I seen a nasty wee chip on his shoulder I said don't worry we'll sort something out as he helped himself to my ciggies I said help yourself he said fuck you mate just shut up and keep fucking driving we stopped off for lunch he said here ya cunt I'm hungry and you're fucking buying I picked up the tab he said hang on pal I want a few beers for the road if I have to listen to you fucking whinging I want a few beers for me trouble.

Since then we've been friends though he's shagged my girlfriend it's weird but I can't help but love him he's stolen my wallet flushed my fish down the toilet and poisoned my cat just for fun he dug up my garden threw eggs at the postman all on the first fucking day he never says please thank you or may I just does what he likes when he wants to he says he likes England now that he's settled sometimes I wish he'd go home but I know I'd miss him his endless bitchin his rudeness his crudeness his manner to hear a wee Kiwi bitch about TV there's shite on ten different channels I said get a hobby he said fuck off I'm busy but busy doing what I don't ask by now I know better the wee bastard's clever smarter than the average soft fruit.

I think Kev's a swinger or even a winger although he once boned my girlfriend perhaps he's just lonely though he's never told me even Kiwi's have feelings I take him out shopping round the fruit and veg section and hope he sees something he likes I'm not sure if I'd cope two Kiwi's in my home shagging in front of the telly perhaps then he'd mellow he is a good fellow but he hates people to know it a feisty wee fucker with chips on both shoulders who loves playing practical jokes on me and my mates in fact just last Tuesday he put glue in both of my shoes before I went to work and when I got home he laughed as I tried to remove them he said don't worry mate I'm here to help I'll even call you an ambulance he's not really greedy just squishy and seedy and always a friend is a friend.

Let your mind go your feet do the walkin your eyes tell a
story and your ass do the talkin in a bouncy castle lookin
for the kitchen flicking back through history to when I was
Egyptian a servant of the Pharo Tut the boy King's mighty
Kingdom the first true great society and all our history's
written in the stones we left behind our legends and our
customs turn the page another age in which I was an
Aztec I think I was a soldier then I know I died in battle
clear but fleeting memories the City of Atlantis lost deep
in the oceans now its secrets gone forever where only
fish walk its streets its corral coated treasure glistens in a
watery dream its Temple tall as Everest streets as wide as
they are long where only sharks do business and the odd
sunken ship her mast dwarfed by the statues.

The view from Mount Olympus was stunning I remember
the human race were chess pieces with which the Gods
played tennis good old Zeus was well amused with our
erstwhile Earthly antics Aphrodite looked quite feisty and
always got her way Eris loved causing chaos mayhem
made her day Jupiter in a drunken stupor made animals
from clay and let them loose on the Earth then watched
his toys at play Neptune always stunk of fish I suppose a
sea God should Ancient Greece a masterpiece its cities
stand today Atlas was on his knees the World upon
his shoulders but he smiled and said I'm fine 'tis only a
wee boulder all the Romans I think were homos before
Constantinople became the Empire's capital that weird
'cause it's in Turkey.

I think I fought in World War Two or was it World War
One all I recall is blood and mud and the deafening
roar of guns I don't even know which side I was on the
Allies or the Huns the Russian revolution now what a
fucking mess the Tsars lost power then their heads the
Communists kicked ass I stood beside Geronimo our
people were enslaved I was a Knight of Christ once too I
died on the Crusades a Viking we will go my boys I lead
a hundred raids I died a sword in my hand I made it to
Valhalla I fought the Boers in Africa we had spears they
had rifles another hero's death for me another short lived
lifetime I was a Kamikaze pilot I must have been a Jap
my plane was loaded up with bombs I saw a ship then
smack a blaze of glory another story another death I'm
back.

But all these deaths are history and here I am again
another body another life another time for men drinking
wine to pass the time and all my heroes dead and yet
I grow and strive once more to do what's just and right
history will be my judge for now I stand and fight and
you my friend where does time end and timelessness
begin where do you draw the line in the shifting sand
can an eon's memories bring you any wisdom can a
leader lead from the front and still defend his Kingdom
can a killer learn to love or a lover learn to kill can a
leopard change his spots or an old dog learn new tricks
where do shadows turn to dust where do nightmares end
where the fuck is morning town just around the bend it's
all uphill come on my son your rest will be well earned.

Enter the Pinball Wizzard all hail the Pinball Wizzard oh fuck he looks like a blizzard get a grip he's a man that is all hold on who dares say just a man that is like one saying just a planet or even worse one saying just a war or why not even say just a species as if that sums it up one wee sentence how can a few words encapsulate the miracle of man at Heaven's gate how can mere useless words ever describe how it feels to look in that man's eyes the fire of creation burning there always one step ahead but not quite there always reaching further than I dare always on the crest of that one wave always braver than the bravest brave always being the one who up's the stakes always being the last to use the brakes always and forever on the make.

Always being the one to cut a path through this crazy fucked up maze through which we pass on our way to what no one can say the Wizzard doesn't care he just plays and the fucker always seems to win instinctively he knows which way to turn with his finger always on the pulse a mind that is refined there's nothing worse than a man who thinks he's living with a curse or always needs his mum to dress and nurse his silly little scratches wipe his arse the Pinball Wizzard smiles now back at us pathetic little mortals scratching dirt while he rides the wind swoops down then soars into the great blue yonder sets his course beyond where any man has been before and follows it no matter where it goes he'll make it there regardless of repose.

Long live the Pinball Wizzard give it up for the Pinball
Wizzard there the fucker goes some new adventure in
pursuit of adrenaline and of pleasure a bungee jump
before he has his breakfast skydiving for lunch then
freehand climbing up some fucking mountain then
absailing down it in one go into a river and in a wee
canoe takes on its rapids tow in longboard surfing is for
kittens the Pinball Wizzard knows that life is precious
and everything he does is for a purpose although he is a
wrecker he's not reckless with his life or health he knows
his limits but he likes to stretch them every minute that
he is alive his mind is thinking of some new wild way to
conquer human fears he sees that as his mission while
he's here for that is when one feels the most alive when
one faces danger and survives.

Pinball as he's called among his friends said to me I'm
going to steal a plane something nice and big like in
an airport do you want to come along it will be fun and
besides I'll need someone to roll me joints we'll fly it till it
runs right out of fuel aim it at a mountain then jump out
so don't forget to bring the parachutes and after we bail
out we'll watch it crash into the fucking mountain what
a laugh I said what the fuck come on let's do it anyway
I've nothing planned this afternoon so we stole a car and
drove it to the airport waited for our chance and then ran
for it and stormed a long haul jumbo set for take-off with
only a few cleaners left on board as soon as they had left
I sealed the doors Pinball fired her up the engines roared
aimed her down the runway and took off.

George kidnapped the malt of the month half ten
Tuesday morning we'd been drinking since Thursday
lunch and just run out of alcohol he said Mike I've got a
hunch if we nip down the offie some dozy fuck will be
working the counter we can just run in and grab it I said
George that's a Hell of a plan but it lacks a bit of drama
if something's worth doing it's worth doing with style
we need another angle firstly I think we should walk in
backwards so the guy will think we are leaving I'll dress
as a woman you dress like a man and we'll pretend we're
having an argument I'll bring a dog you bring a pram
we'll look like an everyday family don't think for a second
I'm holding your hand I'm gay but I'm no faggot ok mate
let's give it a go it's risky but I'm willing to chance it.

The ullage on Hugle's fearsome when left alone with
George sometimes half a bottle and I was only gone to
the toilet we started on Thursday with half a case and
two full cases of Chablis Chablis being the grape I think
from a place called Chardonnay somewhere in the Hute
Medok down the river from Gamay Penfolds now there's
a lovely grape usually grown in Shiraz from which they
make a lovely white wine sometimes sold in bottles
Coats De Whrone is a nice wee town but not as nice as
Shampagne a bottle of bubbles to ease your troubles
and a few bottles more just in case Beau Jo Lay any day
we drink it straight from the barrel and good old Bord
Do as everyone knows is always a top notch tipple here
come the Yellow Bow Tie Brigade leaking wine from their
nipples.

Ah yes the Yellow Bow Tie Brigade of which I'm a lifetime member their Charter states the names of the grapes and what each one is used for Blanks De Blanks is wood made from planks from which they make wooden barrels Maceration is a small Island Nation where they make a wine called Ma Deera Pinot Noir comes from the Loire and usually grows on vines Tempranillo is a wine growing region in the south west of Australia Cloudy Bay in the south of Spain is famous for its Cognac Riesling's Italian but made there by Spaniards the grapes crushed by the buttocks of virgins and after it's frozen its fine flavours are woven into that world famous drink Peas Porter the Bow Tie Brigade state that it's aged for three years then two then a quarter.

Drink while you can drink while you're standing drink while you're falling over drink while you're able to sit at a table drink till you're so drunk you're sober the first time I got pissed I was only six since then it's been a vocation and that fucker George is as bad if not worse the bastard drinks more than I do to him it's religion he's worse than a Muslim he worships all day every day he's got his own cellar of wine that he treasures but all the bottles are empty he claims it's the ullage if so I'm a cabbage but wine is for drinking not keeping you can't take it with you like money it's see through to deny yourself pleasure's a sin let's have a party we don't need a reason you'll sleep all you need when you're dead a man who knows wine whose tastes are refined aye George knows his white from his red.

Mad as fishcakes mad as carrots mad as banjos mad as parrots mad as crackers mad wild bastards I woke up sleepy my dreams were trying to keep me in a soft green wonderland where all the fish were people I thought I seen my house not far in the distance the sky looked quite the same but the land looked slightly different the hills a wee bit smaller than perhaps they should be and windmills by the road they weren't there when I was little everything looked soft and clean I felt warm and safe and happy my rural childhood stomping ground my house down in the valley I could see my Mum out in the yard hanging out the washing I was excited 'cause later I knew she was going to take me shopping and if I was good she'd buy me some chocolate if I was extra good an ice cream.

The road that I travel's an interesting one long since I left my wee home head first into the big bad world young Mikie all on his own I found the world to be as bad as it's big but magic all the same my parents had taught me all that they could and gave me an easy pronounced name most of the people I meet on the way are good people kind people helpful and though my Mum worries for me she believes in a God who protects me I remember my Ma used to ruffle my hair I'd look up like an Angel I remember my Father's gruff bearded smile as he growled from behind the newspaper my childhood made me the man I am now and sometimes I cry I'm so happy the road that I walk is scary sometimes but my ancestor's wisdom still guides me.

Good people you people and I love you all and some
days I meet one who makes it worthwhile the challenge
of living the choices we make foot to the floor or heel
on the brakes have you got the guts to follow your heart
are you man enough to begin at the start and say to the
World I'm naked I'm lost but I'll make it home to Hell with
the cost and what does home mean a place an idea a
memory perhaps of somewhere quite real faded to sepia
tones in your mind childhood reflections the passing of
time old friends with new faces but eyes that remind a
man that he once was an innocent child but far in the
distance we always remain overgrown children locked
in our brains beset by worry but there in your veins your
body is bigger your blood is the same.

Sometimes I feel ancient I've always been here sometimes
a day passes and feels like a year sometimes I sit here
alone at my desk hoping my work's done and soon I can
rest but then I cop on the return of the brock bigger than
ever solid as rock the work pays itself a hundred times
over though always I carry my world on my shoulders yet
each time I smile the load's a bit lighter on the quiet side
of morning I hear the drums beating my heart is revived
the ghosts are out sweeping the shadows of dust from
streets that need cleaning Empires will fall legends are
made but the child that once you were always remains
in your mother's eyes a golden wee saint a bouncy wee
bundle of energy tamed that child lives within you the
world looks the same.

The Hellfire Club were back in town this time with a guest of honour the shabbily dressed but very well spoken Lord Smidgin Whingin De Camp the waiter knew it was a special occasion 'cause they all arrived in their Rollers some of them liked to drive for themselves but Lord Smidgin of course had a chauffeur how's it been boys it's been a while but I'm frightfully busy these days my daughter's just married a Texas oil baron all money and no fucking taste nothing new there chipped in Bag Adeer the Americans are all the same they bought London Bridge now that was a stitch and for England a tidy wee scam what do you think Earl Fallus D'Fink you lived there once I believe yes once in my youth they all were uncouth thank God they all live over there.

Which one of your daughters enquired Sergeant Major Vagina Orgasma or Buttocks I can't quite remember replied the Lord Smidgin my memory's not quite what it was I think it was Buttocks she being the youngest for her dowry I gave them a Castle the one up in Scotland I don't really use it I think the land carries a title the Yank was delighted 'cause now he's entitled to be called Earl Sitton D'Pile the Duke De Munt Gummery spat out his turkey and said Smidgin why did you do that to purse land and title to a Yank with no bloodline a new money American brat your ancestors fought wars to earn them those honours you give them away like mere toys and whatever next who's taking bets that Yank takes his seat at the Lords.

Don't worry Munt Gummery the Yank may have money but nobility's different completely our noble forefathers were legends and martyrs they gave all for their King and their country good old Lord Longford he's dead now I mourned him and men like him will never die their names are immortal their lives an example of how greatness can be achieved clarity purpose energy focus an unshakeable will to succeed will always prevail where others may fail men like Lord Longford exceed what happened to valour our leaders are shallow Churchill the last to have balls a man for his time an Old Empire kind a navy man forged by the sea he weathered the storm of a terrible war and never once thought to give in a captain stands firm his men rely on him that's what nobility means.

Humility's the thing that makes a man noble chipped in old Bag Adeer uncommon these days endangered in places society's weakened I fear why did society evolve in the first place if not for the common good our leaders should lead us yet never be heedless of the needs of the tribe's weakest member protection for all the weak and the old the poor the needy the homeless society's a chain and we're all linked in a chain always snaps where it's weakest what use then the strong ones the chain their in broken pedalling but going nowhere a country should mother its citizens welfare and not just the ones paying taxes for how can a man who works hard and lives well enjoy it while people are homeless a culture of fear builds up in this era but fear of just what I'm not sure.

Striving for humility in a galaxy of ego yet beyond that
Santa's dreaming of a reindeer with a red nose three
times now I've faced my death three times I survived
three times now I've played roulette three times the gun
was loaded three times now I've gambled all three times
now I've won three times now I've lost my mind three
times the world has spun once I heard the Earth vibrate
once I watched plants grow tonight I met the Future
Kings it seemed they did not know the world is theirs
the Kingdom's heirs the past gone up in smoke no bad
thing the slate is clean the future louder echoes calls us
on come on my son two rainbows mark the gateway the
Twin Towers fell but what the Hell these shifting sands
continue looking forward thinking back that boy that
once was you.

What sacrifice would you make what can you give that's
worth knowing that one day everything turns out as it
should change things if you want to man fate is just a
word in the end it all fits in I feel the changeling's hurt all
I've learned I give to you I ask nothing in return I hope
sometime you'll think of me and hope that brings a smile
although sometimes this Earthly life brings only need and
toil the seeds that winter couldn't reach wait just beneath
the soil come the spring life kicks in come the spring
we'll make it endless possibilities endless paths to take us
to that place where freedom's grace strips a bare man
naked and pain is just a memory a loop within a circuit
a tiny thread woven in to the tapestry that makes us who
and when and what we are we're strong enough to
take it.

Strong enough to now stand firm strong enough to walk across a baking fire pit as if it were black chalk strong enough to take the watch strong enough to steer strong enough to take the helm and call the bluff of fear through the storm's very eye the Helms Man steered his course the ocean caved into the sky the storm rolled with its lust through belting rain and flying sea the Helms Man sees a way and carves his path along knife edge waves his eyes calm as his face the ship and him move as one almost like he's surfing the mast is gone the sails are torn the anchor dragging nothing the oceans depths licks its lips in Davy Jones' locker but not this time the Helms Man smiles his goal clear as his purpose many lives rely on him homeward he safely guides us.

Out on the edge of a false night time created by the storm the Helms Man steers her steady now along familiar currents which he knows will take them home while behind him still the storm drags the sky into the sea the sea attacks the sky Mother Nature at her best his ship is but a toy not far off the starboard bow the Helms Man spots a bird and though it is a tiny dot he knows the Albatross by the way it cuts the air he turns the ship to follow and soon the horizon's darkened line can only be his Island his heart expands a tiny tear seeps from his weathered eye the Albatross swoops and soars his kingdom is the sky the Helms Man holds steady his course the coastline of his Island almost seems to reach to him you're home my child I've missed you.

I was talking idle nonsense for a change the cactus I
was talking to thought I was deranged I said hold on
ya little fucker calling me a nutter I'm not the one who's
living out in the fucking desert with nothing else around
except sand and fucking lizards you get fried every day
and have your balls froze off at night time and maybe
if you're lucky some bald fat lazy vulture will come and
sit on you while he chews the last of supper and what
is going on with all those spikes and needles are you
hoping to grow some wool and learn to fucking knit and
if you did what would you do with a jumper in the desert
a baseball cap and shades I think would be more useful
better or perhaps a wide topped funnel to help collecting
water it hasn't rained as yet this year and now it is the
autumn.

And by the way what's your name I'll call you Mescalito
I doubt it really matters much you're a plant while I'm an
Eskimo hang on a sec what the fuck am I doing in the
desert I should be up in the North Pole clubbing seals
to death the last I knew I was sitting on some crazy fuck
named Benny playing cards in New York we lost I think
we legged it but it seems these days it's hard to tell from
one day to the next who I was what I am and where the
next trip ends sometimes I miss the endless ice my igloo
and my husky sometimes I think I'll lose the edge my ice
axe become rusty did you know a polar bear only mates
at Christmas did you know a killer whale only kills when
hungry do you know Emannuel Kant I think therefore I'm
crazy.

All the while the cactus sits smiling to himself wondering if the Eskimo got lost looking for ice looking up looking out for clouds that promise rain it has been such a long year now my reserves are almost drained but I'll live I always did whether it rains or not if there's one thing the desert teaches is to savour every drop life is water though I need little without it I am lost beneath this desert's stone dry ground my roots are spread in search of the barest bit of nourishment this landscape has to give but I'm alive that's a start a start is just enough to maintain a cacti's brock for life though desert life is tough I've seen many summers now in wintertime I sleep and though the sunshine bakes my flesh my roots are cool and deep I know that soon the rains will come and then my roots will drink.

Life it seems is everywhere regardless of conditions life it seems when in need can make its own provisions from ocean depths to mountain tops to deep inside volcanoes the Dragon's breath can be felt ah good old Merlin knew it Crowley got it right that in between a man can't know his left hand from his right somewhere back then when men were men and living all that mattered a mans word was his solemn bond cast iron like his handshake stand by me face front be strong listen in the distance a drummer's solo steady beat begins the future's echo in every corner of the world the dancers will assemble and slowly at first tap their feet until they gauge the tempo every dancers moves unique yet move essential the DJ screams Geronimo the crowd goes fucking mental.

Slap my thigh call me Roger cover me in jam I'm a jammy dodger hold my hand spank my monkey off my tits feelin funky carefree legless cookin up H for me and the man and four of our mates who got fucked who got chucked who bent over who got plugged who died young in time immortal who brocked on who went mental who stayed home who made breakfast the loser wins the player profits the Ice Man melts in fits of laughter the Dice Man rolls a pure weed splitter roll up roll up stand in line twos threes fours passing time changing still yet never knowing where you are where you're going where you're from where you've been what comes next in between on a desert highway lost with no directions no one brought a map and we're running low on petrol.

Where the fuck is my cranium somewhere between my ears and my colon colonic irrigation the latest fad trust me people you've all been had all you need is focus and balance all that matters the drummer and the dance all your futures' in your hands all your pain shadows and dust all your fears lack of trust in the giant that you are come Little One soon not far echoes of infinity you are atoms joined together in a beautiful pattern believe it you're a winner scratch the surface there is the answer heal yourself from inside out don't be afraid scream and fucking shout smash all the barriers break down the walls focus energy clarity balls in the land of the blind the one eyed man is King only cowards hedge their bets and only players win.

The long and final sleep waits patiently for all but in the mean time play to win and have a fucking ball throw yourself a party for no fucking reason just around the bend waits the healing season oxygen is life it's free so fucking breathe it can you touch your toes slowly with your knuckles if you can't you're fucked your body will soon buckle if you can then do your body is your mind strengthen both together the drummer will keep time the human body grows at sixty beats per second into this life we're born and while we're here we're children if you're smart you'll know you'll never know it all if your strong you'll grow if you're a man have balls if you're aware whey hey you're half way there already if you can walk then run if you can run you're deadly a man is a machine a machine that is your servant.

Fighting demons in my sleep I woke up scratched and battered they say your mind makes it real my friends think I'm a nutter out there once I fought the Bear I broke the bastard's nose when he sees me now he runs life's like that I suppose rites of passage I don't know perhaps I never will but if I meet those dogs again I'll send them straight to Hell where the bastards were conceived from Satan's very spawn if you won't fight you pass them on you have a chance so take it while men like Babylon survive Satan is a faggot catch a whisper in your hand squeeze it till it screams naked that was how you're born you're naked in your dreams that's why you never see yourself but demons hurt and bleed there are many other worlds than this in one of them you're King.

Maths is a mystery to simple country kids like me but to some it is a song infinite in tune melody equals harmony Pi is not a pastry MC squared I have not heard the square root sounds quite painful chalk on a blackboard most of it seems a question previses an answer that proves not a lot but most of the things we see think and feel rely on that very plot once I met Elvis reincarnated this time his angle is numbers his hair looked the same but a wee bit shorter he still plays guitar and turns up his collar he sings sometimes but never if you ask him he still loves burgers fries and a milkshake he likes to smoke cigars and drives a Cadillac he always wears sunglasses even in the winter once I asked him why he said son 'cause summer's coming.

Thank you very much the King mumbled through his milkshake shame about the squirrels as he glanced down at the pizza guess they don't like burgers just as well 'cause I'm well hungry Joey grinned then laughed those fucking bastard squirrels nearly had my ass lucky I wore trainers thirty two and a half percent ullage on the pizza muttered George as he poured himself another litre of finest Chablis from Bour Do then gulped as he inhaled it very nice pre drink drink this Chablis Chateau Vintage I bought it on the boat from France I find it's easy drink it although I'm hoping soon we will get down to business how about a bottle of Chateau De Shiraz the ninety eights were very good the ninety nines not bad a baker's dozen every case if not then you've been had.

Hold your glasses Georgie boy we've still got loads of
champers fourteen bottles in the fridge less three we
had for breakfast forty two thirds in total less nine on
breakfast ullage a lovely way to start the day healthier
than porridge and quicker too can you be bothered
turning on the cooker waiting for it to heat then boiling
milk and water then adding half again of porridge stir it
to the boil allow to simmer for half an hour then sweeten
it with sugar or with honey if you prefer or season it with
salt anyway George how about a nip of afternoon malt
just to keep the chill away my old bones feel the cold
autumn's breath is in the air green leaves turning gold
and soon we'll see migrating birds fly south to winter
homes cutting V's through the sky the clouds to them like
roads.

Joey cut a line for me for Elvis and then George a fiver
a go boys cash is clean I'm not doing any tic after all to
get us lunch I risked my fucking neck I heard a car smash
outside I knew it was the Ninja that little fucker could
smell drink even in his sleep two seconds later he came
through the ceiling arms and legs akimbo shouting boys
I think I'm sober 'tis an awful fucking feeling Georgie
boy thank God you're here Elvis how ya doin the King
replied feeling fine been dead but now I'm livin rock on
rock on roll up my son once I was a legend now I am a
nobody another faceless citizen but that's the way I like it
the world just keeps on spinning are we going out tonight
I feel the need to rock and soon every fucker in the world
will know the King is back let's brock.

Half a childhood lost to fear the healing comes another
year passes quicker than the last as now this instant
becomes the past once upon a time people lived in tribes
simple hunter gatherers or simple farming lives survival
was enough safety was a plus it takes a village to raise a
child it takes a village trust freedom and safe keeping and
friends with whom to ruck it's stormy now over England
commuters rushing home worn down by their existence
Pavlov's Dog and bone get up and go to work be a
productive citizen but take a sec look up just above your
heads a tapestry of clouds of every shape and colour
constantly in flux one face of our Mother bless us with
fresh rain fading as they empty the most dramatic part of
a cycle that brings plenty.

Do we appreciate the magic of that mystery can we
stop the clock freeze a second in eternity a still life
of the world through which your mind roams freely
observing everything each tiny perfect detail the beauty
of it all can I describe that feeling in total fucking awe
far past thought or reason awareness absolute every
atom breathing I'd done so many drugs I'd lost all hope
of living through that crazy trip a song sung by Bruce
Springsteen was all that I had left nothing else had
meaning as slowly bit by bit I pieced my mind together
the shadows that had been were gone now gone forever
in the furnace of insanity I forged moulded and tempered
a mind clear cold and strong a mind open unfettered by
the burden of the monkey and the fears of my ancestors.

I felt it in my bones I knew it as a child the world was
somehow wrong some little piece was missing from the
jigsaw that I lived in and without it the whole picture
could never be complete without it all was fractured and
what exactly was it that I searched so hard for to be
honest I can't tell you such things need more than words
but now I know I've got it I'm never letting go each day
reveals some new thing each day its own reward each
day I learn how little I know each day I am reborn each
day the dreams of Future Kings call us lead us on a
species taking baby steps and soon we'll learn to walk
and leave far behind the memories of an epoch marked
by war the burden of living is on us all and we all make
a difference we all know the score we all are magicians.

Each of us play a part and every part is vital to the
harmony of the whole to me life is a battle never let the
pessimists win never give an inch keep hold of your brock
no matter what the drummer gives you strength and
when you're old you can look back and say I played to
win your children and grand children will be strong as
well and proud and if you're lucky you might find love
love will skin you alive break your back break your heart
then mould you anew but this time you will be complete
a whole new real person with a curious light in your
eyes but on this too words are no good sentences cannot
describe quite how it feels to stand at the wheel sail
through the storm and survive are you a player do you
really care or are you just here for the ride.

Fraggles in kilts Smurfs on stilts Leprechauns on mescaline
badgers just out for a swim said a Yank to an American
but wait there's fucking millions of 'em the land of the
free democracy and liberty besieged by badgers battle
hardened and hungry for a feed all along the coast the
Badger Horde amassed Colin gave the nod the Badger
Horde attacked in units of a million led by ten who
were the leaders Colin L'Ancer Turkey Cardigan Shifter
Spunker Trevor Pinkie Milker and Don gained the eastern
seaboard from Miami up to Boston to say that it was
chaos would be an understatement to say that it was
carnage would be more realistic the badgers took no
prisoners they fed like it was Christmas the Americans
taken by surprise they didn't know what hit them.

Reach for the stars reach for your toes what exactly
happened next no one really knows no one left to tell the
tale nobody survived the badgers simply disappeared
where could that many hide perhaps they went to
Canada or even Mexico they could have moved down
to Peru or the forests of Brazil the wilds of Argentina or
to Chile in the hills they might have gone to the South
Pole and disguised themselves as penguins or maybe
Polynesia and scattered through the islands I'd say they
just got tired of war and settled in New Zealand and took
on jobs playing Orks on the set of The Lord of The Rings
could a badger be an actor what does an Ork look like
arms and legs perhaps a head two tone coloured stripe
only J.R. Tolkien knows they came from that man's mind.

Everything we've got all we have created at first must
have existed in someone's imagination keys doors
lampshades cars boxes books bottles spoons tins ashtrays
bins trolleys supermarkets tables chairs bicycles tacks
toasters coasters mats lighters fags needles pins marbles
barbells windows puzzles scales hats wheels chains paint
and lamposts I could go on and list everything that has
been made built or created but that's been done that's
not fun who wants to read a dictionary some people do
off ya go I'll see you in the next life life's too short for
shit like that life's too short to waste in this life you get
one shot muster arms make haste attack your inhibitions
nurture your ambitions and when death comes look
straight ahead or else you might miss something.

Hari Krisnahs masquerading as Buddhists handing out
leaflets and talking utter bullshit Kamikazes dressed
like Santa surrounded by Elves getting pissed on fanta
a snake in my belly a tiger on my back a Dragon on
my mind eyes that glow and wings that flap breathing
fire through his nostrils Dragons are not evil they have
got the power and never can be killed yet they can be
tamed or even be your friend such a magic creature their
beauty is their strength I ride on one in my dreams and
circle distant planets last Friday out past Jupiter I saw
that fucker Benny I think he lost his Eskimo somewhere
in the desert on a far off blue green planet I think they
call it Earth I didn't stop to say hello he looked a wee bit
stressed I sailed on past the Sun then homeward to my
bed.

Friday the Mexican ferret the world's best private detective was working on a case in Scotland looking for the Loch Ness Postman apparently he's been seen every Hallowe'en cycling with his bag of letters across the lake's surface pedalling like a fucker whistling a ghostly tune the Loch Ness Monster called in our hero Friday to investigate this other local legend I've fucking had enough she said to Friday in a huff the Loch is too small for us both the fact that he appears like clockwork every year makes a shitty situation even worse all around the lake people watch and wait if I pop up they barely even notice I've even heard them say never mind it's only Nessie we've come here to see the Ghostly Postman what am I to do I feel like a wee fool a used up old hat legend.

That night the lake was placid Friday dropped some acid he said it helps him think and see things clearly far off in the distance he thought he heard a whistle and was off like a greyhound on a scooter at the far side of the lake the mist was thick and heavy Friday twitched his nose he said I'm sure I smell a pedal that fucking Ghostly Postman won't escape me this time I'm Friday and I always get my man woman whatever that Postman thinks he's clever but I'm Friday the Ferret they don't call me the best just out of kindness then his left ear twitched he knew that in the mist the Ghostly Postman was out doing his rounds Friday had the scent a slight damp letter stench getting stronger as he gave pursuit he knew that he was close his little ferret's nose twitched he thought I'm sure I smell a ghost.

Bit of a mist out tonight thought the Postman on his bike back once again in dear old Scotland and now I have to cycle across this fucking lake again a hundred years or more I've been doing this job delivering post to ghosts through an inter-dimensional hop now please don't get me wrong I enjoy my work ghosts are often lonely and write to friends a lot you see ordinary ghosts don't move around they always haunt one place and to that place they're bound I'm on my way to see the Barber of Inverness a ferocious wee ghost five hundred years dead he gives a Hell of a haircut he'd do it for free and if I stay a while even better the letter I'm bringing is from the Waiter of Ealing they've been pen-pals since they were dead the Hag of Dumfrice is also quite nice though she insists on giving me head.

The Brickie of Bristol gave me a parcel to bring to the Jockey of Leeds on my way back I have to collect a note from the Nutter of Oxford the Rent Boy of Kent is a bitchy wee cunt but is good friends with the Stripper of Bradford a feisty she ghost and when I bring the post she strips off and shows me her knockers the Carcass of Cardiff gave me a spliff to bring to the Melon of Tidwell the Ghost of King Henry is a pain in the nuts he thinks he's still King of the country he gives proclamations to a ghostly dalmatian and when I arrive he sets the dog on me all part of the job it has its rewards I get to meet everybody ghosts are not dangerous they're simply lost spirits who died a traumatic death this mist is quite thick I better be quick or I'll get my post bag all wet.

Look the Devil in the eye and tell him he's a cunt there
might be pieces missing you'll find them if you look when
I was just a boy I went to see the World sure that I could
take it on I left my home to work at that time I knew it
all or at least I thought I did certainty and confidence
just a little kid and truth be told I almost lost I almost hit
the wall but something hidden deep inside heard the
future's call I fought the bastards every step I fight them
still today enemies tearing at the gate growing every day
my mission is a mystery whose fibres somewhere hide a
grain of truth a piece of youth now love is on my side the
burden of humanity the world upon my shoulders at that
time near broke my back but now I'm old I'm stronger the
first one standing on the walls the first to face the danger.

Stronger sharper faster clearer all's on fire all's a mirror
all the animals all the fish all the birds make one wish all
the children sparky eyed bringing forth the healing tide
all your fears all your doubts bullshit shadows burn them
out the supernova that you are can't be stopped you'll
go far there's never been anyone quite like you follow
your dream make it fucking come true smash your telly
burn your bridges there's no going back no way of telling
what the future holds for Elvis Me or Joey ask us do we
care do we give a fuck strap me to a rocket I'll take a
chance good luck to all you magic people who read this
little book you're capable of anything you're real you're
strong hands up this world needs heroes come on boys
and don't forget your brock.

Don't forget to make the tea don't forget ya bastard don't
forget a man is sober that is until he's plastered naivety is
not an asset nor indeed is guilt does anyone need a cross
to bear a sword sunk to the hilt honesty is where it's at
be honest with yourself the Guardians still believe in you
that's why they hold the fort the hands of a healer hurt
the most a rather strong smell of smoke drifted to me from
the kitchen some cunt was burning toast we were running
low on pizza the party had just started Brendan returned
dragging a wheelbarrow filled with cans of lager it's
much less trouble than making tea he muttered to no one
listening their eyes were glued to the unusual sight of a
flying television fill your glasses come on boys to Hell with
lunch get drinking.

Call the cops call a corpse call a pigeon a bastard call
a shovel call a spade the call of the wild is louder to
my ears than the call of suburbia revved up spotless
Landrovers aiming their way aimlessly to the carpark at
Marks and Spencers a disused phone box tells the time to
people as they are passing the short brock uphill through
the graveyard to home down by the station the sound of
my shoes on gravel the tunnel of no return out the far side
still in one piece it's downhill now hold it together your
brock will soon see you home face the pain for beyond
it is pleasure these steps I know lead somewhere that
I've been before perhaps many times these steps seem to
shrink as I grow the key fits the door and slowly it turns as
staggering I made it home.

The ending of an era the beginning of an eon the
Wizzard rolled another spliff and passed it to Fen Lon
so tell me boys he said as he smiled has anyone seen
Urban Jones the last that I heard Riley replied he went
off to find Babylon complete waste of time said Ninja
in rhyme he should have sent Friday the Ferret Friday is
busy said the Ghost of King Henry he's doing a job up in
Scotland working for Nessie I'll bet it gets messy hey Joey
cut me a line you owe me a tenner Joey replied I don't do
credit for ghosts just then the door opened in walked Four
Commandos and said boys it looks like a party put on
the kettle said Hansel to Grettle the Three Little Pigs killed
a wolf beer is for breakfast said Big George to Pockets
whisky now there's a man's drink.

What happened the pizza said James Joyce to Nietzsche
they'd just popped in for a chat could have been squirrels
badgers or pigeons I reckon meself 'twas a cat who gives
a fuck said the Hellfire Club in unison from the sofa wine
is for women Big George was bitchin hey Mike serve
up some brandy hold on a minute said the ghost of Phil
Linnot first port then brandy then smack all in good time
Michael replied as Pinball sparked up a spliff the ghost
of John F. said what the heck I'm dead but my name is
immortal the ghosts of Kurt Cobain Jim Morrison and
Stalin played Russian Roulette with a chicken the prize
was the pleasure of fucking at leisure the corpse of
Marylin Monroe I'll have some of that said Schrodingers
Cat as Einstein said here we go.

All these dead bastards 'round my house plastered
George Bernard Shaw in the kitchen trying to divide four
fifths of a pizza between nine ghosts ten drunks and
a chicken watch out for the toaster I said to the ghostly
ghost of the Lock Ness Postman twixt the sink and the
fridge a portal exists that leads to a lake up in Scotland
don't worry Mike as he straddled his bike I'll use the one
in the bathroom madness is natural sanity's casual the
echo's of fear can reverb as loud as they want but one
stubborn cunt looks fear in the eye and grins back a race
of dead horses run rings round the courses specifically
designed to confound them the seagulls on steroids the
pigeons had flick knives while outside my window they
battled.

The Ninja and Joey split hares over anchovies most of
which were called Karnack a tin of sardines a pocket of
beans a tube of luminous face paint four drunk drugged
up fucks got in a ruck over the German expression for
soufflé sou fley ach bin housen Cowboy was shoutin as
Big George countered suf-lay fuck you said Pockets in
Deutschland they pronounce the a s and u not the f you're
being colloquial said Pinball though joking there was a
Kraut in my family tree along with a junkie a rocker a
punk a raver a mod and a hippie some branches some
leaves a trunk and a bark although we hadn't a dog
carrying sap straight to my bap displaying a landscape
of leaves this shit's a good hit as George passed a spliff
back to himself via George 2s 3s 4s and 5s all brushed
aside it's 6s I think thank you boys.

Gourds on every side and none of the fuckers cooked follow the shrew follow the shrew one hit and you're hooked one taste you're an addict the Gods rule the Planet yea it rained it fucking rained I made it by a minute all my friends my mad fucked up friends you're Gods and you don't know it focus focus fucking focus focus is where it's at the staggering simplicity it rained and you got wet a storm straight off the Atlantic swept over southern England and any poor fucker caught out that night got it the storm took no prisoners trees were flattened buildings were battered cars were turned over power cables knackered Mother Nature kicking ass give an old dog a new bone do you know what you're capable of can you find your way home.

Holy Fuck it's nearly Christmas Santa is cumming so is his missus the Elves and the reindeer were getting it on Rudolph in leathers a mask and a thong somebody told me reindeer love carrots now I remember it was Friday the Ferret can a ferret be classed as a person Friday can he's nicer than most the last that I heard he was chasing a ghost my mate's on the run so help me I helped him here's one thing for you to remember a friend is a friend is a friend now and ever your friends are your real strength without them you're nothing you can't choose your family you don't even have to like them your mind is a tool use it at will explore it expand it we're numbers in constant flux in constant free fall where philosophy becomes maths and truth is in all.

Somewhere a lighthouse exists in your mind its faint
but sure beacon reflects in your eyes at the still point
of knowing all becomes one two that I know of one yet
to come and though it may take a lifetime of learning
I'm calm and I'm patient I live every second I know if
I try I could see the future that's not why I'm here fore-
knowledge is useless as is reaction at the still point the
pattern reveals completely each tiny wee fraction a piece
of the jigsaw fits into place a clue to the mystery an
emotionless face I'm only just starting I'm just being born
I screamed for my freedom as they cut the cord my hands
are like anvils my back broad and strong I've learned
what I know the learning goes on bring me your demons
I'll show you they're weak a man's an expression of life
at its peak.

You are what you eat you are what you wear you are
your expression your voice and your hair you are a
wee minnow you are a big fish you are a mad bastard
you are what you wish you're a phenomenon a real
life Poke-Mon a hero a King a fugitive on the run from
stupid little men with tiny little minds but soon we will be
strong enough soon we'll turn and fight soon we'll show
the bastards just what we're gonna do soon we'll make
them stop and think we're fools what have we done we'll
turn this world upside down arse upon its head the kids
step forth to take the lead and all the pessimists dead
it's party time come on boys the beat is in your bones
the dance floor shakes creaks then brakes the DJ's head
explodes the roof caves in the sky's on fire through space
our fury echoes.

The ugliest omelette in the world was out that night on the pull I fancy a bacon sandwich he thought or perhaps a vindallo he was feeling good his hair slicked back wearing his new suede shoes in his back pocket four new ribbed small condoms duck fat a pliers and a bottle of fiercely strong poppers he'd nicked from his mother's personal supply of uppers downers in-betweeners sleepers pain killers and tranks she would never notice he knew 'cause he always did this on Friday night if she ever woke up it was Wednesday with luck she'd then head straight for the doctor's doctor doctor I'm in pain I need strong drugs for my brain I simply can't take it I smile but I fake it the real world is cold and it's hard the world's ugliest omelette was hard and up for it sure that tonight he would score.

He booked a taxi into the City downtown please driver he said out on the pull the driver enquired just shut up and drive the omelette replied and fast the night is a wastin the first bar he hit was an ocean of tits not bad he thought to himself I'm sure to score here unless they're all queer if so they might let me watch some lesbian action a pleasant distraction these slippers are goers for sure I've heard that a dyke will go like a bike she just needs the right man to cure her he strolled to the bar and ordered a cocktail a Sticky Blue Murphy please barman the barman just laughed and said are you mad it's lesbians only tonight the omelette said shit just my fucking luck turned and walked to the door on his way there a dyke like a bear gave him a kick in the crotch.

Out on the street he gritted his teeth in pain but not going
to show it I know what to do I have to get screwed I'll go
to one of the strip clubs just four doors down was Officer
Brown's he was sure this place would do ten quid at the
door he bitched at the whore who charged him but paid
her anyway I don't give a fuck a buck is a buck it's worth
it if I get laid inside was dark he stood by the bar and
surveyed the talent on show up on the stage the dim light
displayed a woman fist fucking a sheep and there by the
curtain he seen he was certain a postman being chased
by a ferret interesting show he said to the person stood at
the bar beside him is this your first night came the reply
as the stranger turned round to face him maybe babey
why are you asking do you fancy a shag and a pizza.

It was love at first sight stood just to his right was an
ugly ham and cheese toastie do you come very often
his opening question was a winner he knew it for sure
only at orgasm replied the ham toastie tell me are you
on the pull who me why no never he was being clever
an omelette plays hard to get I've seen you before
somewhere 'round here so do you fancy a fuck or what
your place or mine the toastie enquired fuck it let's do
it right here they climbed up on stage the audience
cheered as the pair got down to business the girl and
the sheep finished their bit the spotlight turned on our
hero he whipped out his weapon the toastie was drippin
the audience applauded the sight the world's ugliest
omelette's pre-coitial display the best thing on stage that
night.

I seen my own reflection walking backwards up the stairs
I seen my death my burial my gravestone but who cares
I seen a genius clutch at straws I watched him as he fell
his palms were scarred by slipping shards his blood was
fresh and red I looked into his eyes as he hit the rocks
below they spoke one simple message as death claimed
one more fool every second's fucking precious every
breath your last every moment you're alive's a bonus
you can bet your ass simplicity's the key to greatness
sensation's first and last if you can then fucking do the
past will be your judge don't spread don't hedge don't
hold don't fudge don't give away your cards don't think
or blink don't smirk or flinch just play as best you can it
doesn't matter what cards you have just how you hold
your hand.

A Devil sat across from me the dealer in the shadows I
knew this game was life or death the prize that night my
soul a poker face I drew an ace the bastard seen my aura
my Father's voice came to me be calm my son you're
all right I bet the lot twice the pot call a bluffer's bluff
win or lose we can choose but do we give a fuck I've
been through worse but never said please stop enough's
enough the dealer passed out two more cards one for me
and him one face down one face up who dares who bets
who wins what price these days a pound of flesh what
price a pint of blood what price these days your sanity
see through paper stuff the dealer said come on gents
closed bets show your hands and as I turned my cards
face up I watched the fucker dance.

Blood from a skeleton I won the pot the lot a Devil
scratched the ground for clues I laughed you're fucked
ya cunt winner's walk loser's talk dealers know the score
cash your chips count your tips the loser gets a whore
I cleared the table said good night gents and legged it
for the door quick decisive value common sense above
genius poise or wit one sure thing a winner knows is
when to fucking quit out of town heading south boot
down all the way some new fucked-up adventure I'll
live another day a cheeky smile another mile that Devil
had to pay for every game of cards has rules and only
players play every game of chess needs pawns don't give
the game away as sure as daytime follows dawn and
nightime follows day confidence is all you need can one
man take the pain.

Can one man see beyond the lies using only human eyes
to who knows what and who knows where the ticking
clock as time passes TV the opium of the masses as
nightime brings a gentle peace the answers come the
questions cease energy its own release shadows dust
atoms water human beings bricks and mortar as all the
pieces fit together and one man says it's now or never
the power of tears the gate to Heaven opens to a man
who's willing to gamble every fucking shilling lay down
his life if that's what's needed the stakes are high so are
the winnings strange flashing lights mysterious sounds
repetitive beats dancing clowns the drummer smiles
oblivion calls ecstasy crumbling walls the pressure keeps
on building the gambler counts his winnings.

In search of the Philosophers Stone I walked the northern coast Atlantic storms ripped my ears and told me I was lost how many times I walked the beach until I ran out of sand and had to turn back and face the long trek sore feet and empty hands if I was lucky I'd find a shell and wonder where it came from deep in the Indian Ocean perhaps brought here by a sea storm my Father's a sailor or at least he was for twenty years or more and sometimes these days I look at the sea and know that out there's my home out past the islands I could chase the sunrise if only I had a boat but then nightime rises for me here on dry land but the night skies bring its reward far too self conscious to take it all in the sky at night makes me feel small.

We used to fly kites down on the beach we loved it when there were storms Pete could paint a picture with a twelve foot sky tiger the kite was his brush the sky canvas the colours were chosen by his facial expression and changed tone with every move strange sepia sadness as the wind briefly died down excited as it returned that echoed in oranges lime greens mixed in tangent with the purplest purple I've seen when he really let go those same colours would glow like street lights from under his skin the pattern not knowing where when why it's going a pivot that's all Big Pete was his feet cutting the ground eyes rinsing the sky in search of where to go next a low sea tide lifted some sand as it shifted the water line slowly onshore.

One half step ahead is better than dead air half way up
on the lift in a turnpike I happened to be there I doubt
if Pete cared he spoke to the wind that he played with
shadows and dust invisible gusts of force four high winds
on a good day 'tis strong from the north though I expect
'twill get worse all hands on deck untill we reach port
a mere indigestion the weather was having our ship's
strong the keel made from oak seasoned and tested sharp
sure we rested our sails on the way home while tides
as familiar as the smiles of our children brought us safe
home to our Island on its northern coast the sand dunes
play host to echoes of sea winds that carry the dreams
of all sailors out there on adventures with strange tales of
pirates and treasure.

Safe home with his family a sailor on dry land is just like
a fish out of water his eyes search the skyline he senses
it's soon time to take to the boat once more the comfort
of home the safety and warmth feel shallow to life on
the ocean the ship under full sail her keel cuts the sea
borne by the trade winds south by south east to pick up
a cargo somewhere in India and trade for tobacco north
then to Holland a cargo of silver we have to deliver to a
merchant over in Boston from there then who knows north
south east west home that is the life of a sailor riding the
high seas the trade routes like our streets at night time the
stars are reflected by the oceans pale silver a flickering
mirror a carpet of diamonds emeralds and pearls these
are the things that we sail for.

Have I watched the changeling bleed I've been there
once know how it feels now and then I can almost
remember being sixteen going out playing hurling or
our all time favourite boyhood pass time good old stick
fighting climbing trees climbing walls fishing with nets
robbing orchards ringing the church bell to see if we got
caught looking cool hanging round corners gettin into
fights after school discos always skipping mass never
missing school 'cause that's where all your mates were
and you learned the basic rules of organised society
that didn't always work but you made the best of it and
tried to make it fun conker season apple fights loyal to
your gang a good and simple life oblivious to the outside
world our village was enough our village was our home.

Our play was governed by the seasons in summer time
we'd swim the river in autumn time the annual floods
changed the landscape so we'd make boats or else make
rafts that usually sank on their maiden voyage but we'd
just laugh everyone had bicycles but no one ever bought
them we used to make them out of parts and hope they
held together at harvest time the haybarns became our
number one adventure building camps building tunnels
getting chased by farmers they wore wellies we wore
runners climbing up the water tower another favourite
sport from the top you'd see for miles we'd point out
our own houses down the town the Castle grounds was
a high risk proposition to sneak inside climb to the top
always worth a mission.

The simple things the little things these are what's
important simplicity is where it's at simplicity first and
foremost how many senses have you got say five then
you're a jackass how many senses can you feel now
there's the fucking question everyday insanity everyday's
a blessing every day could be your last this is how to live
the greatest power that we posses the power to forgive
humility humility humility's the key a straight cold gaze
at this strange Earth where somewhere we're all free how
lateral is your thinking or do you wear linear blinkers just
how far are you willing to go to prove you are a winner
gotta push the boat out gotta take the plunge gotta
achieve focus Annie get your gun I've always known
which way is north and when to fucking run.

My mother is an Angel kind patient and selfless I am
proud to be her child and every day I prove it if I ever
hurt someone I too will feel the pain there are no outside
agents watching every move but everything's connected
everything's a groove so giving is its own reward you can
so give you'll win energies multiply energy's the key when
you give it multiplies giving is a feed kindness is a virtue
a virtue that is free I'd walk through fire for you my friend
if that's what you need a random act of kindness very
rare these days 'cause most of us are blinded by others of
our race most of us are shallow and hide behind a face
that can watch another suffer and not reveal a trace most
of us live in fear that fear that has no face.

Aimlessly I walked around the environs of my new home town Sunday morning afternoon first head north out by the schools turning east up the hill the Sunday drivers out to kill anyone and themselves I'm glad I walk the roads are Hell down the corner the scooter shop closed down now the bikes all gone a building site where I turned right heading south some friends pass by and wave to me so I smile back not far on I hang a left east again into the park Sunday families in the playground the little chiefs charging round my step picks up something's close I'm not sure what follow my nose a downhill path there in the grass the thing that I've been looking for a perfect symmetrical natural wonder the still point's close I can almost touch it.

Scanning the ground totally focused the still point's here I fucking know it stop inhale there it is I almost blinked but I know it's real frozen to the spot unable to move time completely stopped there in the still point's groove the answer to a question I'd been asked years ago if you had been walking by and seen me crouching there you would have said that guy is nuts you would perhaps be right you could have hit me with a brick I doubt I would have noticed the still point had me by the balls total fucking focus there and then it all made sense the last five years of madness that day I fell from the sky and somehow fucking landed in a field on my feet the Universe a rabbit ran headlong between my legs how could I understand it.

Twenty three twenty four the still point clicked through its trapdoor I fell head first then five years later I found myself back on this Earth a crazy fucked up magic planet spinning round a fading star that looks at times vague and familiar I think they call it Sirrus Major I'm not sure but who needs details if you think life's complicated find the still point perhaps you'll make it lots have tried most have failed they got stuck in that Groundhog Day don't be fooled don't be led you're not a sheep you have a brain some guys call it Russian dolls some forget but some find more some survive others don't some run away some lose the plot some get confused some get lost the still point's there it takes no prisoners no idle strays no weekend wonders.

I love the smell of garlic I love the sound of rain I love the taste of mushrooms I felt the changeling's pain I love the feel of soft stuff I love to look at nature looking back at itself falling through a trapdoor there I seen the building blocks that made up the first layer short sharp straight lines acute angles intricate folding tangents simple basic pure design set in slow motion where measured time is pure nonsense you are alive but are you conscious you are aware but can you feel it you've got two eyes but can you see the truth behind the mystery the still point's calling me I hear a far off distant future dance floor echo to the beat of hardcore where people wearing cyber gear partied non stop for a year the future happens now the future happens here.

A bastard pikie Somoan vegetarian who refused to eat meat but loved the taste of chicken spent most of his life living in Crawling a biological experiment which then became a town filled with vegetarians Kevins Trevs and clowns the experiment was started way back in the fifties a team of so called experts set out to build the perfect chicken out of everyday materials you might find in your kitchen cling film tin foil old egg boxes knives and forks ceramics Teflon a wooden spoon two bread baskets four tea strainers wash-up liquid household cleaner scouring pads a mop and bucket a weighing scales a whisk and a strainer washing powder seafood chowder pickled onions freeze dried burgers instant coffee tupperware tubs non-stick pans and rubber gloves.

They wanted this chicken to lay the perfect eggs up to fourteen hundred a day and all a perfect size square eggs round eggs flat eggs oval eggs a nice smooth brownish shell with white and yolk inside the biggest argument they had was what to fucking call it Harold Gerald Donald were just a few suggestions but someone said let's build it first and simply fucking ask it you see they wanted this chicken to be able to talk sing and dance do the splits do algebra and walk a tightrope trampoline play guitar do the house work drive a car tend the garden iron clothes do the shopping on his own use a type writer or a phone be an economics wizard never eat and live forever even replicate itself from one of its own eggs an androgynous asexual PC perfect hen.

Of course it didn't work the chicken went berserk it
started laying pairs of shoes and then it got the hump
when someone said hey listen Fred you should be laying
eggs the not so perfect chicken had chosen his own
name and said to all the scientists it's my ass and I'll lay
anything I fucking want so then they built a cage and
tried to make him live inside but he got out the first day
little did they realise that Fred could fucking fly at almost
twice the speed of sound two foot off the ground in a
flurry of feathers he was off like the clappers never to
be seen again by any of his inventors Fred went on a
pilgrimage to try and find himself bit of a mission for a
self aware chicken made of cleaning fluids and delph
how many years he walked the Earth alone aimless and
lost.

Many years later Fred gave up searching he decided to
settle down he laid enough bricks in a couple of weeks to
build a whole fucking town south of the city down in the
country he began to construct his new home he called
it Crawling an urban mess sprawling with roundabouts
dead-ends and houses that all look the same then people
moved in most were called Sharon or Kevin the Adidas
track suit was cutting edge fashion and everyone there
drove a Nova not a bad place to live in compared to
the slums around Mexico City Crawling's an example
of poor social planning you see people are people not
robots square pegs and round holes will never work nor
will round holes and square pegs people are people New
Towns can not equal the heart that exists in a village.

What's a belly button supposed to do on the last day of
October the clocks have turned back the afternoon brings
a foretaste of coming winter Hallowe'en night the Eve
of All Halo's a festival to honour the spirits the spirits of
summer return to their slumber the spirits of winter take
over time to reflect though not with regret another year
reaches its closure the harvest is in we've stocked up with
wood and stored all we can in the larder it's time to rest
the land takes a break the trees have less leaves every
day stark but proud creatures reveal their true features
their frailty belies their true strength deep in the earth
their roots rest and wait patient quiet and powerful part
of the earth they've broke solid rock they know that each
year they get stronger.

Sit close round the fire I'll tell you a story to keep the
dark evening at bay a long time ago on my Island home
a sailor came back to stay he married his sweetheart
bought them some farmland built them a house with
his hands a quarter of a mile from where he spent his
childhood his own children were born four bright eyed
strong children who lived by the seasons and worked
every day on the farm they learned about nature to love
her and tame her and respect for all living things he
taught them that springtime is when to get sowing and
hope there won't be a late frost and then early summer
to watch tend and nurture to weed to thin out and to trim
and then come mid August prepare for the harvest the
work was about to begin.

Early September hope for good weather it's time to bring in the hay harvest the beet potatoes and wheat the smell of dark food yielding clay will always remind me of an amazing childhood you see one of his children was me I look back sometimes and think of that child covered in muck wearing wellies a simple existence going out picking mushrooms our hens provided our breakfast in our little front garden we grew parsley and carrots long beans lettuce and thyme we had gooseberries rhubarb blackcurrants raspberries and cabbage though I didn't like it my Ma was the gardener my Father the farmer and between them they kept us all busy there's work to be done get out of bed son cereal with hot milk for breakfast then out to work the frost showed my breath as my Da fired up the tractor.

A wee Massy 20 World War Two tractor most days we had to push start it when she got going we'd just keep her running when revved up it sounded like thunder eight acres of land the back of my hand I knew every stone every furrow my Da built the haybarn that was our playground with slides swings camps jumps and tunnels my Ma would get worried in case we got buried under a few bales of hay my Da would just laugh they're not made of glass they're children and hardy wee fuckers but mums always worry and sometimes we got hurt but it was only wee scratches or bumps that were easy made better by some love and a plaster a pat on the head off ya go that place still exists where that little kid and his Da still work on the farm.

A wolf in sheep's hotpants a mixture of circumstance
old friends returning new steps but the same dance the
pleasure of learning the challenge of living caught in a
bubble I knew I was spinning somewhere outside sirens
were ringing but in here it's quiet the drugs have just
kicked in do you remember that strange sinking feeling
oblivion calls there I go willing I've been here before but
each time it's different in some subtle way sometimes the
picture just paints itself invents its own colour chooses its
form finds its own structure right then I'm a pawn but who
is the player right then this means nothing layer on layer
of fact strip away revealing fresh air a handful of sand a
wing and a prayer time is a joke that's lost in the telling
numbers are rumour the answers compelling.

Knowledge is useless words facts shit fruitless the end
is in sight but can you get to it choices dilemmas cross-
roads to nowhere the trip's just begun you wished it was
over I'm loosing my grip it's time I just let go the bubble
expands bang there goes my ego my first taste of air my
first taste of freedom my first cigarette my first drink my
first fuck all history now perhaps I'm a grown-up but what
does that mean whose keeping score who stamps your
cards who pays the bills can you accept that life itself
kills who knows the future who gives a damn who knows
what's important who pulled off a scam who came out
laughing who came out at all who went to bits when they
hit the wall who covered all bases who hit a home run
who got left behind who missed the pun.

Where's me tobacco who's got me skins roll up roll up
the show must begin bring out your dead bring out your
living the show must go on bring out your kitchen call
up your heroes call up your mates it's Friday night the
weekend awaits don't get complacent don't get blasé
don't get too fucked don't run away don't chicken out
never give in don't stop the healing don't stem the flow
act don't react don't say till you know don't think till
you're sure a man is a myth a myth is a show the show
has just started you're in the front row half empty half full
half past half way there half human half dream half joker
half player half man yet half mouse half measures are out
in for a penny in for a pound play till the last hand play
till you're broke play till you're dry play till you choke.

Play till you're lost play till you find that shadows are
dust dust that's refined to hold some strange structure
that looks real but shines with a strange translucence
that somehow reminds a man he's a myth a myth that
defines the sound of the wind invisible blinds slightly
fogged up keep out the draught though it's in my mind a
man is a myth until he decides to tack to the wind a wind
that provides all that he will need to grow and survive
my roots still dig deeper there somewhere outside the
bubble an echo faint but alive sounds like my heart two
three four times five eleven hundred and seventy add one
decimal point to the picture and zeros trail off to the right
to numerical infinity $Ez=y$ while fifteen years later one
man takes his time a beggar gets rich an immortal dies.

Atilla the Hun missed the pun Hitler called it quits Bob
Geldof is the only man I'd really like to meet somewhere
a jukebox plays cheesy tunes classic 80's hits that all hold
emotion memories of teen-hood time capsules of when
they're released melancholy sometimes I am but always
in a nice way echoes of moments that made me a grown-
up echoing things yet to come keys that send shivers right
down my spine tingles across my scalp flash-backs a
time-lapse fast-forward then fast-back for an instant two
moments are one with no in-between this I can't explain
you know it accept it that's all just like Deja Vu I don't
have a clue the strange the wild and the weird all keep us
guessing searching and learning I suppose that's just part
of being human.

Who says impossible the fools lazy dossers with as
much brain power as a turnip the pathway to learning
is everyone's birth-right have you got the balls to admit
you're a drop in the ocean a grain in a sand dune be
smart don't get lazy don't quit don't criticise don't close
your eyes when you see something you know can't be
real accept it and learn be placid be calm be water be
fluid be a sponge the Kingdom awaits just step through
the gate onward and upward my son out here time is
lost a shadow of dust a trick of the light an illusion in
this faker's world we think far too much clarity's all that
you need ego's a lie built to disguise an insecure man's
needless fears but don't believe me jump head first you'll
see the water's your friend all along.

Sometimes I got dizzy flying my kite sometimes I got
lost in the movement sometimes the kite chose its own
course as it carved the sky over the sand dunes the great
north sea winds carried a taste of the Arctic Iceland and
Greenland me and Big Pete dug in our feet as we battled
a force six that Wednesday strange that I had completely
forgotten till Karl reminded me of it but so much goes
on for this mad wee man how could I remember it all
but that place in time will always exist although the tide
swallowed our foot prints our kites can be seen reds blues
pinks and greens dancing in air passing children looked
up in awe and begged for a go we always said yes
then we'd teach them a couple of minutes they were the
experts their wee faces glowed like the sunset.

Stormin tea cups irrational fuck-ups head banging
walnuts free falling doughnuts symmetrical puzzles
inside-out boxes that can but don't contain themselves
outside the space within cracking knuckles infinite
numbers twisted sisters even more twisted brothers fuzzy
logic lateral thinking tonight I watched a player bet and
watched a player win flickering street lights abandoned
buildings strange but subtle nuances strange but simple
beings strange but normal circumstance strange but
stranger things strange how one's reflection carves upon
the glass an almost perfect figure and you can bet your
ass that your eyes are filters filters through which pass a
blinkered scaled down version of a world bereft of flaw
where all is truth in beauty and one for once is all.

Wh'ell it's a one for the money two for the show born to go crazy and walk every road born to go wild born to go schizo born to break even and get buried in a hole born to learn born to run born in pain born to have fun born without a name born without a clue born to play the game and break every rule born to be addicted to every passing fad hooked on every drug and thrill that I have ever had living for experience the new the cool the daring living life on the edge sometimes I lost my bearings and though I always made it back sometimes the way was painful my feet had never left the path a fool I didn't know it time is such a silly thing time often disguises time is simply relative to how you choose to spend it time can be your master your bitch your whore or servant.

And yes I think the world is fair in some strange fucked up way each of us must earn a crust and each must pay his way each of us must learn the price of all the things we value each of us must do what's right and each of us must carry the burden of humanity and all its dreadful sins out here players chew the bit out here players win out here magic's every day out here solids melt out here shadows made of dust fade away what's left open canvas brand new paint a virgin brush a faint impression of raw energy an echo of a time when the world was pure and yours you see time's in fact a lie the little things the simple things the stupid things but why is a man a masochist albeit in his mind perhaps we are born inside out we know we're born to die.

Don't ask me for the questions you won't believe the answers don't ask me for directions 'cause I'm as lost as you are don't ask me to remember I've done too many things to try and point to one and say my life changed 'cause of this I've smoked too many fags to say perhaps some day I'll quit I've seen too many layers strip away to think that I will ever see them all look up look down don't blink and man sometimes my arms bend back my memory plays tricks on itself but what the Hell memory's a bitch a bitch that only serves itself a bitch was I to think that I fucking knew it all when I was just a kid a kid who would take on the world take on the world and win vacant eyes passing smiles naive thoughts mixed in with something that I learned before before I played to win.

The sound of air rings to my ears the sound of home revolves the sacrifice I make sometimes sometimes the bravest calls a bluffer's bluff a bluff's in truth a wall that's only fucking made of brick built by man how tall justify the mirror-man live by the rise and fall learning what it means to bring an ocean to its knees learning what it means to hurt to love to grow to feed learning from my memory and everyone I meet learning without knowing learning without judging learning without thinking learning cataloguing learning is addictive learning's where it's at become a sponge absorb it all you did when you were tiny all the things you've seen changed you from a blank page to a person and when you close your eyes you'll sleep 'cause sleep's the bravest journey.

Evil wears a shallow mask be smart you'll see right
through it set yourself the highest task who knows you
might get to it certainty when it comes will give your life
more purpose in seeking out the fallen ones who don't
enjoy the Circus a fly on the ceiling holds no meaning
unless you are the fly your life will change subtly sprayed
on layers of time variables change constants won't and
through you all these filter the stories you learned when
you were young with time perceptions differ our clouded
grown-up blinkered world leads into a labyrinth isolation
dead ends frustration moulded plastic faces like the
people you see on the trains out like rats at the station
glad to be free from the stifling air ignoring the situation
play with your laptop all by yourself digital masturbation.

Nobody's perfect nobody's imperfect nobody gives a fuck
nobody will help you is that what they tell you if it came
to a ruck no Santa at Christmas no leaders just dick-
heads boys with big toys running countries no passion no
vision no true grit no wisdom no balls no brains just bad
hair no genuine concept society's complex from up there
you can't see a thing puppets to business driven by profits
we're human or have you forgotten down here life is
different it won't fit your blue-print your think-tanks your
census your polls will teach you nothing society's rotting
and politicks is at its core you claim you can rule us then
lead us don't fool us don't pull the wool over our eyes
don't play to the press don't make us guess and last of all
don't feed us lies.

Where light bends 'round corners and fragments of
stardust flicker out of existence there once was a planet
green-blue what was it don't ask me 'cause I'm just a
drifter I think I'm a comet but from where I'm sitting I
can't see if I have a tail but if I am that's not too bad
man there's worse things to be here in space I could be
a nebula a red dwarf a small moon a freak or unique or
a dream the Milky Way's pale light fades out of my sight
in some way's a cute little galaxy nice for a weekend
or an afternoon's shopping for adventure I head for the
edge to watch gas giants explode leaving a core that
might become black holes sometime creatures of gravity's
hungry reality swallowing light time and matter I'm
tempted to race in to see what would happen perhaps I'll
try it tomorrow.

A world trapped in crystal sits on my table reflecting
refractions of patterns such cute obtuse angles woven in
tangles the still point sits on its axis and inside a rainbow
shows me the way home but home is wherever I am
kaleidoscope meanings echo my feelings layer upon layer
upon layer of self induced notions and no magic potions
can tell you just who what you are a creature a mammal
the son of a camel herder or are we just fiction dreamt up
in our dreams reality's seams stretch out of recognition
liquids to solids lost shopping trolleys under a railway
bridge filled with dead wrappers programmed consumers
filing in two by two to buy all the latest symbols of status
objects gadgets and junk that in some ways own you
what can a man do a paradox of one.

Green beans with teeth melons with feet anchovies with
ears wearing slippers cotton socks worship the box
imagery poetry passion memories keys do you think that
bees know that we nick all their honey cigarette buts who
gives a fuck accuracy fallacy nonsense the Land of The
Free an Island of Dreams floating drifting consuming a
smile says it all well done man good call but could you
do it again strange rhythm loose patterns the Ghost King
sang backwards as he fucked the Ghost Queen on all
fours deeper steeper sharper fiercer would you bend
for a friend would you give it all the future will call and
echo your name if you know it the world's a small place
can one man erase all of the things we inherit uncharted
waters lambs to the slaughter better call Friday the Ferret.

The bastard's in Portsmouth off his tits on good drugs the
whites of his eyes red and shining lost walking home his
feet know the road I think he owes me a fiver out picking
cherries wild fruits wilder berries farming fish with a
tractor smoking raw eels heads up the wheels of time turn
faster and faster rhythm emotion perpetual motion energy
synergy fire de-lay-ed-re-action innocence shattered the
world is a bitch so bitch slap it can you take the pain
and carry your name don't flinch don't blink just enjoy
it don't criticise you may realise the monkey's a myth do
some acid no pain no gain no busses no trains no taxis
no rickshaws no trams decide what you want then excel
it everything's neutral everything's beautiful everything's
everything else.

Everything turns everything burns everything is for a
reason everything happens space-time got flattened by
Benny as he made for Saturn light speed by two the joker
the fool the wisher the thinker the corpse the dreamer
the screamer the shadow the healer the sower the reaper
the dead the living the giving the power of forgiving
the power of forgetting the past ambition contrition the
human condition how low can you go can you last until
the end out of my mind shadows behind the dust of
the future unfolding where pain is a game and echoes
remain to remind us just why we believe and why we
carry on the words to the song why we draw breath
every day why we were born why lovers mourn in love all
things come true catch a star make a wish look in look
out be a fool.

Hookers givin freebies cops creating crime left or right
can't decide flip a fucking coin pregnant mums doing
drugs heroin yea fine once I was a blackbird once I gave
a marble to the Gods of the sea a long shot high stake
gamble once I asked the world why me I never got an
answer I've seen the future they call them the Free Boys
there out there biding their time their eyes are different
their facial expressions are kinder they don't need the
scars each thousand years the species jumps forward the
Free Boys the next in that cycle I hope I live to be three
hundred and three the Free Boys might live even longer
their home is called Sky Town and they have no leader
no government no laws they don't need them they've
each got just one name and each different talents the Free
Boys will remake the game.

In a parallel Universe you wrote this and I read it in another place in time a Postman and a Ferret chased each other through my mind standing in my kitchen busy doing my ironing talking to a midget who I think lived in my fridge and ate all of my biscuits antique idle ornaments shimmered in the lamp light my good old friend the Dragon tree told me he was thirsty a magic landscape sailed away I woke it was eight thirty have to go to work again so what it keeps me sober for a few hours every day my livelihood's a burden that I carry willingly the pay is shit but fuck it every member of the tribe contributes to its progress except the village idiot a harmless mixed up unit time in loops hula hoops Rubric's Cubes and turkeys that are bred to stuff themselves with haggis shoes and burgers.

Once again the Moon's near full my nipples are like bullets mes tetons sont durs comme des boulets ou est ma bicycletts je voudrais un billet pour Pari my feet were getting wet as I walked the River of Dreams clichés back to back who made that perfect wooden sphere and painted on a map who ordered rare beef wellington the Hellfire Club are back the waiter smiled he always did the wine was getting warm put it in the microwave put it on re-frost the Ugly Duck laid massive eggs that grew up to be swans never waste time on regret self doubt or idle pity 'cause when you get down to the bones the true grit nitty gritty vision is a memory your eyes too slow to see it are you proud to be a man a woman or a ferret are you strong enough to stand while all disintegrates.

Who will miss me when I die who will give a fuck who
will bring flowers stand and cry seal me at last in muck
will they sing a hero's song or beat a sad tattoo with
every mirror's dream revealed you are me I'm you when
I die mourn me not my life's been good and happy but
bury me with my arse to the sky so that passers by can
shag me please don't give my grave a name the flowers
will not care just leave a simple epitaph A Man Who's
Dead Lives Here plant on that spot a conker tree lose
yourself come back to the first line parallel Universe
where white is white not black can you play the guessing
game can you beat the odds far-fetched complex
simplicity freefall flying frogs off their tits on ecstasy
become the wheels the cogs rinsing off infinity raining
cats and dogs.

The mirror said man life's a dream in speeded up slow
motion where everything contains itself and gravity's
a notion that can only justify itself on a solid planet's
surface and yes I watch the changeling grow from a
shadow to a man and yes I felt the spider's web and
backed the also ran and yes I gamble everything and
yes sometimes I lose but does a player give a fuck and
does a player choose the nature of the game he plays the
game's a play where whos what becomes why when if
not the pot contains everything you'll ever need it never
pours it rains did you crash land volley backhand can
you see the traces of fingerprints long gone now the Free
Boys smiling faces always make the game worthwhile a
smile like that's contagious.

Like mercury it falls through my fingers the jigsaw that
was once a picture cartoon people cartoon features
cartoon plots cartoon future's cartoon colours cartoon
meanings cartoon endings cartoon beginnings cartoon
living cartoon politicks cartoon ideals cartoon philosophy
who the fuck are Tom and Jerry Scooby Doo and the Pink
Panther the clues exist although their tiny insignificant
bright and shiny pebbles in a massive quarry that you
will find if you're lucky they may find you if you're patient
bide your time and count your blessings once again
my eyes drift skyward searching for the future's outline
mirrored in the stars vague patterns a map exists your
mind's a canvas stretched out on a wooden trellis that
you've made your choices endless.

Once I looked down from a mountain and saw the whole
world every person looking up their eyes a question
looking in where shadows darken shades of truth a
man's uncertain till he dies if he's immortal that's the
game that's the gamble every facet every angle every
triumph every score every loser every whore every witless
brainless shithead meathead arsehole fuckwit dickhead is
in fact a fallen Angel carving out their vision of Hell every
man for himself women children wait till last orders boys
it's kicking out time the barman rang the bell a second
time a sail that's made of broken promises filled with
wind of whispered curses horror terror fear and loathing
the future's bright the plot unfolding piece by piece frame
by frame take no prisoners play the game.

On this small strange fucked-up Island I soldier on each
day a challenge to maintain a hold a me brock I drink
too much but what the fuck and would you really trust
your doctor if he said I'm sorry it's terminal cancer you've
got non-operational you're going to die get with the
programme nothing makes sense no one makes progress
no one breaks even no one ever wins do Cardinals
commit Cardinal sins sleep when you're dead sleep when
you win The Kangaroo Army The Badger Horde ferrets
chasing ghosts pimps chasing whores around my head
logic for breakfast cigarettes for lunch drugs for supper
the land speed record is meaningless in air the future
doesn't give a fuck the future doesn't care I love these
quiet evenings I love the taste of air.

I love this growing madness uncertainty abounds I love
the English language 'cause words are shapes not sounds
I love to push the boat out I love to push my luck I'd love
to take you to the edge and then watch you jump I love
when things are shrouded in mystery and doubt in the
middle of the maelstrom I heard the changeling shout
why was I born human if in fact I am perhaps we are all
dolphin's dreams living on dry land perhaps we're all
immortal perhaps we're walking dead perhaps we are
all numbers in some crazy fuckers head perhaps we are
a virus perhaps we are a myth virtual reality a computer
game for kids on some far off planet I think therefore I
am what the fuck does that mean perhaps there is a plan
to all this magic madness believe in what you can.

I've started so I'll finish not that long ago I stared into
the mirror and watched the changeling grow and yes
I took the red pill there is no fucking spoon how could
there be a dark side behind that grapefruit moon subtle
indications subtle cryptic clues subtle connotations subtle
disguised moves to some half imagined afterlife win
break even lose your mind if you want trust me you don't
need it and yes you might think I'm a cunt a reckless
fucked up egitt do I give example do I give a fuck in this
world there is one law and that one law is love I used
to read books all the time looking for some answer till
my Father said to me you won't learn much from books
I thought I was immortal I thought I was a King I knew I
was a player a player born to win.

It's half four in the morning everyone's asleep through
night time's hazy curtain I feed off people's dreams
perhaps I've never met you perhaps you are my friend
perhaps we are all minnows in this stagnant urban pond
perhaps this book's a figment of your own imagination
perhaps a player gambled all and won his own salvation
I think Fen Lon rolled a spliff and smoked it all himself
I'm sure Big George nicked all the booze fucked off and
got pissed the Hellfire Club were cooking up heroin in
batches I tried to give up smoking instead I gave up
matches the middle classes lost the plot it's tricky in the
centre Joey said hey Mike fuck off a squirrel's a fearsome
bastard half them carry flick knives half are Kung Fu
masters.

The little things the simple things your mind is not a
prison raise your head you will see the light beyond the
tunnel read the papers watch the news play loud music
play to lose a man cannot escape himself cards face
down place your bets every thought a silent echo all your
fears shifting shadows made of dust in sunlight hollow
somewhere a promise carved in stone flawless letters
edged in gold Kurt Cobain sold the world and took the
easy option perhaps that was his destiny perhaps it was
the shotguns will a puzzle really care if you never solve it
and will its solving change the world as history dissolves
it will its solving bring you close to the child within 'cause
in the end that's all that counts growing old is sin the still
point's at the centre that's where you must begin.

What a fucking sunset it took my breath away I know
that is a cliché it happens every day some lucky people
in a plane saw it from the sky burning brilliant beauty
can make a grown man cry but I didn't bother instead
I smiled and nodded to the greatest artist ever as he
cleaned his palette painting west as the sky filled with
cloud spun Dragons once a man nailed to a cross
forgave the ones who did it random things random
beings random pathways home random truths miss spent
youth random idle gestures random people that I meet
old friends new friends strangers home is where I lay my
hat but I haven't got one I dreamed I lived in Sky Town I
dreamed I had forgotten I dreamed a perfect ending to a
strange lifelong adventure.

Mirror's mirror filter's filter the brave stand on the walls be brave enough to hear and heed the future's distant call I've found that life finds its own pace regardless of one's efforts to jump the gun re-hash the past or play off cards not dealt yet if you can remember that time when just four things existed sound rhythm motion and warmth though you did not know the words yet at the front of your mind a patterned white light awareness pure and simple de-programme re-programme new programming language that's what we need here comes the new breed we're bringing a brave new world with us this fast changing world is not fast enough we care far too much for tradition the questions are simple the answers plain English the new breed are here on a mission.

Go get 'em my son the game's just begun don't be afraid of the shadows 'cause that's all they are echoes of fear that build up in layers on your forehead they're not set in stone just skin flesh and bone pliable malleable changing the Three Little Buddas know more than I could guess between them they know everything but they don't say they just work and play harmony balance union but their eyes belie the knowledge they hide behind carefree wide smiles and soft features my love for this world has brought me tears more times than I can recall a man's word is his bond a King's castle his home true wealth is having true friends the more the better 'cause each one is a teacher believe me I've been through the hoops where matter dissolves all things evolve and time skips itself round in loops.

Once we were happy wearing our nappies what did
we know then that we've lost simple sensations subtle
vibrations learn all you can then move on a long time
ago I could not say my name before I got hold of me
brock security purity imagined needs self belief hard
work hard times hard knocks hard life hard trials foot
sore miles hard drinkin free thinking endless journeys
impossible mazes occasional glimpses cryptic phrases
hidden meanings emotionless feelings cold clear answers
to unasked questions in an unknown language that
just keep you guessing hard bargains shifting margins
difficult choices long shot gambles impossible angles
T shaped U-turns non-existent corners split second
warnings the dance has just begun it's a long way till
morning.

The last mile's always risky it's when you let your guard
slip with the finish line in sight it's time to break all
records lose yourself in the moment don't think about
your lap of honour keep on learning keep on guessing
keep on pushing keep on testing keep on trying if there's
one lesson that I've learned it's simply this fire burns
some things change some things don't something ends
something starts something dies something killed it but
in the end it all contains a sameness where have I been
where am I going what was it I learned out there beyond
the edge of knowing what of my future what of my past
ignoring spiky pebbles as I walk barefoot on my path to
that cloud bound distant hilltop where I might just rest at
last sit upon a stone enjoy the view and smoke a fag.